Meditations for·Happy Christians

" If God had believed in a permissive society, he would have given Moses ten suggestions."

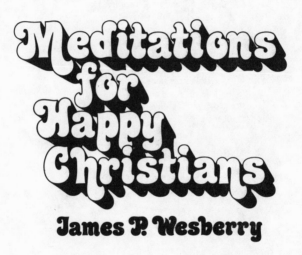

Meditations for Happy Christians

James P. Wesberry

BROADMAN PRESS
NASHVILLE, TENNESSEE

Trade edition: 4255–21
ISBN: 0–8054–5521–3
(BRP item code: 4282–25)

Dewey Decimal classification: 248.4
Library of Congress catalog card number: 72–90035
Printed in the United States of America

Preface

An atheist once heckled a minister's sermon, saying, "If I had had the making of the world, I would certainly have done a better job than God."

"For the time being," the preacher replied, "would you mind making a rabbit, just to establish confidence?"

If we had had our way, we probably would have made a big mess of things. Haven't we already proven that to some extent?

In all ages man has sought the "Islands of the Blest" where there is no suffering, pain, trouble, hardship, or sorrow, but no matter how long he seeks, he will never find it in this world.

It is so easy when the sledge-hammer blows of life fall upon us to be bitterly resentful or to become martyrs. But there is scarcely a more futile waste of life's precious emotions and energies than self-pity.

The troubles of life, whatever they are, have to be borne. And this fact calls for what we might call "creative acceptivity." When life's hardships are gracefully accepted, they may in turn become creative. They may develop new spirits within us, making us new men and women.

It is my hope that the messages in this book will both cheer and challenge its readers, helping them to gracefully accept both the good and the bad which comes their way and turn it into something creative.

James Whitcomb Riley put it this way:

It hain't no use to grumble and complain,
   It's jest as cheap and easy to rejoice.
When God sorts out the weather and sends rain,
   Why, rain's my choice.

We might never be able to *make* rain, but we can make it our choice.

Contents

Meditations for Happy Christians

I

A Good World After All

"It is amazing what human beings can stand when they are fortified by faith in God!"

These are the words a pastor wrote to his congregation about his baby.

"He is physically healthy, and expected to live indefinitely," he said; "however, mentally he will remain a child as long as he lives. He is one of nearly 5,000,000 Americans who are mentally ill. Three per cent of all babies born in the United States are in this group. Medical science cannot determine the cause of this condition, and doctors and educators have children of this kind. Dale Evans wrote a book called *Angel Unaware* about hers."

What is one to do when he faces such a tough situation as this? This fine pastor said, "The only satisfactory approach is the search for the good that might come out of it." He further added, "When we count our blessings, we find that they far outnumber our disappointments, and it takes both to build a strong faith."

What beautiful words these are! They remind us that the apostle Paul was convinced that the things that happened to him were for the furtherance of the gospel.

An unknown poet tells us that this world is a curious compound:

With its honey and gall,
    With its cares and bitter crosses
But a good world after all,
    And a good God must have made it.

Yes, this world is indeed a curious compound of light and shadow, joy and sorrow, pleasure and pain, sin and righteousness, good and bad, achievement and frustration; but what a difference it makes when one's life is fortified by faith in God!

A British missionary, Allen Gardner, served alone in the Antarctic. He watched for many weeks for a supply ship to arrive. When it finally came, his body was found under an upturned boat along with his diary, revealing his last recorded words: "I am overwhelmed by the goodness of God."

Once marooned on drifting ice in Labrador, facing what seemed to be certain death, Wilfred Grenfell sang:

> My God, my Father, while I stray,
> Far from my home in life's dark way,
> O teach me from my heart to say,
>   Thy will be done!

When we learn to live and serve in the will of God, it is simply amazing what we can stand.

There is a way to make the most out of everything. May God help us all to find it.

2

The Anger of Love

There is much to be angry about today.

Commonly accepted standards of right and wrong have broken down.

The city of New York obtained a temporary injunction preventing the publication of a certain book. The judge who granted the injunction was satisfied that it was obscene; but when the city sought a permanent injunction, the judge in that case declared the book was not obscene. When the city appealed to the appellate division of the state supreme court, three of the five judges declared the book obscene and two said it was not.

For lack of common standards even our courts are often reduced to confusion and absurdity.

This is true in many other areas.

One of the world's outstanding religious leaders says, "We are yellow. We sit while others shout. We compromise while others communize."

Wrong public opinion is created by default because good people say and do nothing.

It is the shouting people who help to create the public opinion and community standards which make a nation great. What a tragedy that so many people are tongue-tied!

During 1961 and 1962 we spent $1.11 on crime in our country for every dollar spent on education. From 1957 to 1962 venereal diseases among adolescents rose 130 percent. After 1955 the illegitimacy rate tripled, and we were warned if the present trend continued there would be ten million American children born out of wedlock by 1970.

One of the big surprises to many people who read the four Gospels is that Jesus Christ, the most perfect man who ever lived, on several occasions displayed anger. If you have any doubt, read Matthew 23. His love for God and reverence for his Father's house impelled him to drive the moneychangers from the Temple. His deep concern for man caused him to be aflame with wrath against inhumanity to man. Love by its very nature is antagonistic to everything that is evil and works injury to life. In every case Christ's anger was the anger of love and grief.

Whatever arouses the slumbering fire of anger in us, let us make sure that our anger is Christlike. Christ is the gentle Shepherd of the sheep, but because he is the Good Shepherd he is the relentless foe of the wolves, robbers, and thieves.

If we forget his anger and hatred of that which is wrong and become incapable of indignation in the presence of corruption, we become ineffective witnesses.

The anger of Jesus is the anger of love.

3

Happy People Are God's People

William Lyons Phelps, long-time professor at Yale, many years ago wrote a little book entitled *Happiness.* Its sales soared, and in five years there were at least twenty-six printings. It seems that everybody wants to be happy but, as Dr. Phelps pointed out, many do not know how.

"There are people," he says, "who carry their happiness as a foolish woman carries a purse of money in her hand while walking on a crowded thoroughfare. The first man who is quick with his fingers, numble with his feet, and untrammeled by conscience, can and will take the purse away and disappear with it. He will have separated the woman and her money. Now if one's happiness is like that, dependent on an enemy's volition, on a chance disaster, on an ill wind, and any one of a thousand accidents to which we are all exposed—then happiness can be lost."

Have you lost your happiness? How many happy people do you know? God's people should be the happiest people in the world.

In every bookstore throughout our land we find tables prominently displayed that feature inspirational books having to do with the art of happiness; but, as someone has pointed out, "All the sages said is in the Book our Mothers read." The Bible teaches us what other books cannot about how to "live a new life," "how to stop worrying and start living," how to have "the mature mind," "peace of mind," "release from nervous tensions," and "confident living."

Take a look, for instance, at Psalm 34. We find many reasons hidden in this gold mine of divine truth why God's people should be the happiest people on earth. Let me point out seven of them. God's children should be the happiest people in the world because:

1. All their thoughts are established.
2. All their fears are banished.
3. All their sins are covered.
4. All their prayers are answered.
5. All their enemies are scattered.
6. All their needs are supplied.
7. All their future is assured.

Fannie Crosby is known and loved around the world for the many beautiful hymns she wrote. She went blind at the age of five and lived to be ninety-five. At the age of eight she wrote:

Oh, what a happy soul I!
　　Although I cannot see,
I am resolved that in this world
　　Contented I shall be.
How many blessings I enjoy
　　That other people don't!
To weep and sigh, because I'm blind,
　　I cannot, and I won't.

4

Responsible Self-Managers

"Why is it," asked a highly successful businessman of his pastor, "that I can manage my business so well and at the same time cannot manage my own life?" This is a question that concerns many people. The answer is that it is easier to manage a business than to manage oneself.

One business executive hired the best accountants, the best production and sales managers, a top tax consultant, secured the best possible advice from efficiency experts, and left no stone unturned to become a wise manager of his business. He knew all about running his business but was unable to control himself. He was irritable, tense, miserable, and unhappy. He flew off the handle at his wife, his children, and his employees. He used profanity and imbibed freely. He became an alcoholic. He had an important job and a big salary, but life lost its meaning for him. Having all, he had nothing because he had no control over himself.

Many people are like that. The road to self-management is a rugged one, but the results outweigh the efforts. God tells us that "he that ruleth his spirit [is better] than he that taketh a city" (Prov. 16:32). The main reason people fail in life is that they have failed to master themselves.

No person can become an effective self-manager without accepting responsibility for himself. The growth of the disciples began when they asked, "Is it I?" All of us need to take a look at ourselves. He who would rule his own spirit must shift gears from the ego to the altar, from himself to others, from sin to Christ, from self-centeredness to Christ-centeredness.

That distinguished English scientist and preacher Henry Drummond was once riding with the driver of a carriage who had been demoted in life because of a bad habit. The driver told Drummond that this bad habit was bringing him closer and closer to ruin. "What can I do?" he asked. Drummond answered, "Suppose this team of horses should become frightened and run away and we were in great danger. Suppose you knew me to be the most expert horseman in the world, well able to handle any horse however wild or out of control. What would you do?" "Why, sir," he replied, "I would instantly put the reins in your hands."

"Certainly," said Drummond; "then why don't you put the reins of your life in the hands of the great Expert on human nature? You cannot overcome the habit by yourself. Why don't you let Christ take the reins of your life?"

No man can exercise self-mastery until he himself is first of all mastered by Christ. Then he can say with the apostle Paul, "I can do all things through Christ who strengtheneth me."

5

Look in Your Own Back Yard

On the banks of the Indus River lived an ancient Persian by the name of El Hafed. From his beautiful, comfortable cottage on the hillside he could look down on the gleaming river and out over the glorious sea. His fields and orchards yielded plentifully. His beautiful wife and lovely children shared his wealth.

One day a Persian priest came to his cottage and told him how diamonds are mined. "If you ever had a diamond as big as your thumb," said the old priest, "you could purchase many farms like this; if you had a bushel, you could own the whole country."

At that moment El Hafed became poor. All of his possessions seemed to lose their value. "I must have a mine of diamonds," he said to himself. "What is the use of spending one's life in this narrow sphere? I want a mine of diamonds, and I shall have it."

He could not sleep. He rose early the next morning and went to the old priest and asked where he could find diamonds. The old priest told him, "If you go and find high mountains, with a deep river running between them over white sand, in this white sand you will find diamonds."

So, enthusiastic, restless, and dissatisfied, he sold his farm, took the money, and went in search of diamonds. He searched through Egypt and Palestine. The years rolled by and at last, after going through Europe, broken-hearted, ragged, a hungry pauper, stung with humiliation, and crushed by bitter disappointment, he threw himself into the Bay of Barcelona.

The man who purchased his farm led his camel out one day to

the stream at the edge of the garden to drink. While the camel buried his nose in the water, the man noticed a white flash of something glittering, glistening, sparkling at his feet. Out of curiosity he picked it up, took it home, and put it on his mantle. One day the same priest who had visited El Hafed came to visit El Hafed's successor and noticed the flash of light. In amazement he exclaimed, "Here is a diamond! Has El Hafed returned?" And the two men went out into the garden, stirred up the white sand, and found diamonds even more beautiful than the first.

Had El Hafed remained at home and dug in his own garden, he would have been the wealthiest, most honored man of his time.

This story tells us that the richest diamond mine in the world lies at home, within our own personalities. If young men or women would have strong, well-trained minds when they reach maturity, they must make much of their mental strength in their youth. And youth is never at its best unless it is strong in the Lord and in the power of his might. Youth's glory is not only in physical strength, but in mental, moral, and spiritual strength. Young David could say to Goliath, "Thou comest to me with a sword, and with a spear. . . . I come to thee in the name of the Lord of hosts, . . . whom thou hast defied" (I Sam. 17:45). His trust in God kept his heart strong and nerves steady, so that even in the presence of a roaring giant he was "able to sling stones at a hair's breadth and not miss." The victory was won by spiritual forces.

To every young man and woman in America I would say, "Look in your back yard. Dig deep. And above all, 'Remember now thy Creator in the days of thy youth' " (Eccles. 12:1).

6

Men Who Cannot Be Bought

Have you heard it said that every man has his price? This is a lie, and Satan is the author of it. Rudyard Kipling once said, "No price is too high for the privilege of owning yourself."

Some men do sell out for money. Judas Iscariot was one of them. He started out a promising young man but wound up saying, "What will ye give me, and I will deliver him unto you? And they covenanted with him for thirty pieces of silver" (Matt. 26:15). How tragic it is to be sold out by one whom you love and trust.

What a striking contrast there is between the man who sold and the man who was sold—a contrast between thirty pieces of silver and death on a cross! Jesus' life was a bright light which made Judas' deed look dark indeed. Judas was purchasable. Jesus was not! His highest loyalty could not be bought for anything less than the will and purpose of God.

Do you see what I mean? Men today are inevitably caught in the swirling currents of life's duties and responsibilities, and the world's demands and pressures threaten to crush them. Is it not required of us that we be unpurchasable men—that no price be high enough to win us from our faith, integrity, and obedience?

This is the kind of man for which God calls today.

What kind of man are you?

God give us men who cannot be bought.

7

The Answer for Life's Loneliness

"FLOWERS GOOD MEDICINE FOR ILL, FARMER HAS FOUND OUT," was the striking title of an article which appeared some time ago in a South Carolina newspaper. It carried a picture of a farmer standing proudly in his flower garden by the side of beautiful dahlias which grew taller than he. Another picture showed row after row of lovely flowers with the man kneeling in the midst of them.

The story related that he had probably brought more sunshine into the hearts of the sick of that area than any other man around. A retired farmer, this seventy-nine-year-old lover of floral beauty and mankind had for fourteen years been taking his flowers to the sick and unattended in hospitals in nearby towns. Three times each week he would carry huge boxes of flowers to the hospitals and go up and down the corridors, sticking his head inside doors for a quick word and a smile of encouragement as his flowers were delivered. He had received messages of thanks all the way from Maine to Florida.

Proud to call Charlie Galloway my cousin, I wrote to congratulate him and in a few days, I received a letter telling how the day before he had visited a crippled children's home, a nursing home, a foster children's home, and three hospitals. "What a joyous time we had!" he wrote.

"How did I get into something that so few Christians care about? Only heaven has the answer," he said. "I just can't stand the thought of someone lying there sick in a hospital bed without friends and flowers. Sometimes they lie there for months with never a soul to visit them or send them flowers."

Here was a man who could see that in sharing his talents and his blessings, he had been the one to reap the rewards. Is it any wonder that he could write, "This has been the most joyous year of my whole life. I have found the answer for life's loneliness"?

8

Can Life Be Made Over?

When we become depressed or discouraged over the sins of the world, the best thing we can do is turn back the pages of God's Book and read once again the story of the potter and the clay.

The mighty prophet of old, Jeremiah, had lost confidence and courage. His heart was broken over the sins of his people. He saw his beloved nation going straight to irremediable ruin and turning a deaf ear to all warnings.

Because of his discouragement God sent Jeremiah to the potter's house to learn some very important lessons. There he saw the potter take a lump of dirty, ugly clay and slap it on the wheel. As the wheel revolved the potter's hands worked their magic, but something happened. The vessel was marred in the potter's hands. But he did not throw it away. Instead, he took the broken piece of clay, placed it on the wheel, and once more with artistic hands shaped the clay until it became a thing of beauty.

This was God's answer to Jeremiah's despondency, to Israel, and to us. God was simply saying that life *can* be made over.

What a message! It deals a death blow to those infamous twins, fatalism and pessimism. Fatalism says that forces beyond our control determine our destiny. Pessimism tells us that man is only an ape with a college education, and asks how anything of abiding value can be fashioned from such imperfect clay? But God says that both fatalism and pessimism are liars, for man need not be hopeless; life can be made over again. "O house of Israel, cannot I do with you as this potter?" asks the Lord (Jer. 18:6). "O Jeremiah," he says, "you need not be downcast, disheartened, or discouraged. Remember what the potter did! I can do the same. Be hopeful. A marred vessel can be remodeled. So can human beings."

Ages ago a potter in Greece decided to make something beautiful. He took clay, put it on the wheel, and fashioned it into an urn. On the urn he put youths, maidens, gods, goddesses, forests, streams, a mountain and a citadel, and a little town by the sea. The urn was sold to a wealthy Greek to adorn his home. The sculptor died and so did the man of wealth. The urn passed from age to age and finally was lodged in the British Museum. There one day a livery stable helper by the name of John Keats, with the fire of genius in his heart, looked upon that urn and wrote a famous ode:

> Thou still unravished bride of quietness,
>> Thou foster child of Silence and slow Time,
> Sylvan historian, who canst thus express
>> A flowery tale more sweetly than our rhyme.

Out of an ordinary piece of clay Keats brought the immortal "Ode on a Grecian Urn," which will last as long as the English language.

Out of the clay of human beings, the heavenly Potter molds vessels of beauty and usefulness, if they are completely yielded to him.

9

Driving the Golden Rule

One of our leading lawyers, the son of an outstanding minister, recently said, "I have never heard a pastor say anything about the Christian's responsibility for good driving."

There are over eighty million automobiles registered in the United States. According to one of our traffic court judges, there were more than three million men, women, and children injured and thirty-eight thousand killed in automobile accidents a decade ago. The figure may have doubled by now.

In a research study entitled "Death by Driving," Dr. Alfred Mosely of the Harvard Medical School tells us that there are 104 deaths per day by automobile accidents throughout the year. There have been only five days in ten years, this report informs us, when less than 100 persons have been killed in such mishaps in the United States. This is indeed appalling!

The fact that "the life you save may be your own" is enough to cause us all to give much thought to our driving. With more than one hundred people dying in automobile accidents each day, we should be able to see that the lawyer was absolutely right. We are not only responsible for ourselves but for the lives of others. We have a direct responsibility to Almighty God for the way we drive. There are many places where we may put the Golden Rule into practice but no better place than on the highway.

Perhaps we all need a reminder. Some time ago I pasted this little prayer in my car near the driver's seat: "Dear God, I promise to drive my best where Thou hast placed me, as the safety and future of others depend on the skill and care with which I think and conduct myself behind the wheel."

"As ye would that men should do to you, do ye also to them likewise" (Luke 6:31).

10

Christianity and Civilization

To adequately express the influence of Christianity upon civilization in the little space we have here would be impossible, since multiplied thousands of volumes have not exhausted the subject.

In nineteen centuries Christianity has gathered over eight hundred million followers. What has caused this phenomenal growth?

The answer plainly is: CHRIST.

Christ is to Christianity what the soul is to the body or the sun is to the solar system.

Christ's resurrection from the grave attested his miraculous birth and atoning death. With the authority and power of the resurrection Christianity spread like fire over the face of the earth. His disciples have gone everywhere bearing the glorious, good news of forgiveness of sin through Christ.

Without the influence of Christianity "Old Glory" would dissolve into anarchy. What a dark and dismal world this would be if the voice of the pulpit were silenced; the schools, colleges, and universities influenced by Christianity closed; and the power of Sunday Schools and youth organizations blotted out!

Who would like the job of taking Christ out of art, or poetry? What man would like to go with chisel and hammer and remove every reference to Jesus from the tombstones of our world? Without Christ, hospitals would go, modern medicine would be paralyzed, and many of the world's masterpieces of sculpture would topple. Who of us would care to live long in any community where there was no church?

It is indeed true that all the armies that ever marched, all the navies that ever sailed, all the air forces that ever soared, all the kings and queens who ever reigned, and all the congresses and parliaments that ever governed have not influenced civilization as Jesus Christ has.

He said himself, "And I, if I be lifted up from the earth, will draw all men unto me" (John 12:32).

II

He Took Our Place

Great and noble are the causes for which men have died. Stephen was stoned to death for Christ. John the Baptist and the apostle Paul were beheaded for his sake. Tradition tells us that Peter was crucified upside down.

What a candle Latimer, Ridley, and Cramer kindled in Oxford Square as they gave their lives in his service! Savonarola and William Tyndale were burned at the stake. Socrates and Polycarp were great martyrs, one drinking the hemlock and the other being mauled to death by wild beasts.

Each of these, and all other martyrs, gave their lives beautifully, bravely, and sacrificially; but none of them died as Christ did. Of none of them can we say as we do of Christ, "He died for our sins." No one else was ever good, great, or worthy enough to die for the sins of mankind.

Jesus set his face steadfastly toward Jerusalem, determined to die, because he knew that by dying all who believe on him would be saved from their sins. What else in all the world could have been important enough to require such a death? Yes, others have died, but only Christ died for our sins.

He died, the just for the unjust, to bring us to God. "Our sins crucified the Lord of glory. Our evil tongues maligned him; our unclean lips defouled him; our palms slapped him; our fists beat him; our sins were the thorns that pierced his brow; our sins were the scourges that made his flesh raw with gashes and red with blood; our sins were the nails that pierced his hands and the spikes that tore his feet; the hammers that drove the nails and the wagging heads that mocked him."

Was it for crimes that I have done,
  He groaned upon the Tree?
Amazing pity, grace unknown,
  And love beyond degree!

But drops of grief can ne'er repay
  The debt of love I owe:
Here, Lord, I give myself away,
  'Tis all that I can do!

12

Beyond the Death Line

At first Kagawa was just a young Japanese student, studying at Princeton. But a few years later when a doctor told him he had only one lung and four months to live, he became a different man, and one the world would hear of.

What would you do if you had only four months to live?

Kagawa gave himself to the poor, to drunkards, thieves, and outcasts. He thought and lived for them. They turned to him as their guide, friend, and hope.

He told the story of his life in a book entitled *Beyond the Death Line,* for he did not die at the end of four months. He never thought of dying; he thought only of living. He was too busy to die, and he lived beyond the death line. More copies of his book were sold than of any other book in Japan at that time. Everybody wanted to know about the man who forgot about himself and found himself.

He became the great labor leader of Japan and was said to have been one of the greatest Christians in the world. Kagawa could say, "He must increase, but I must decrease" (John 3:30).

This is what Paul meant when he said, "I am crucified with Christ: nevertheless I live" (Gal. 2:20). There was a moment in the apostle's life when he attended his own funeral. It was on the road to Damascus. When Saul of Tarsus was converted he was called "Saul," which means big, important; and he *was* all that. But a few years later we find him referred to as Paul, not Saul. Do you know what the word Paul means? It means little, diminutive. Here we see the whole principle of the increasing Christ and the decreasing self worked out in the reality of man's life.

Have you ever noticed how at one point Paul said, "I am the least of the apostles" (1 Cor. 15:9), and a year or two later he said, "[I am] less than the least of all saints" (Eph. 3:8)? Then a little later he wrote that among sinners, he was "chief" (1 Tim. 1:15). This is the glorious doctrine of a decreasing estimate of oneself.

Many of us need to go to our own funeral. It is not a place of mourning, but of joy. If we would be delivered from self and have Christ live in us, we must die to ourselves. It may be painful business, but out of death comes life. In the measure that we are willing to die to ourselves, Christ is able to live and to reveal his life in and through us.

> There is a foe whose hidden power
>   The Christian well may fear;
> More subtle far than inbred sin,
>   And to the heart more dear:
>
> It is the power of selfishness,
>   It is the wilful I;
> And ere my Lord can live in me,
>   My very self must die.

13

The Only Thing That Counts

One of the saddest pictures in all the world is that of old King David standing at the gate, waiting for news of his wayward, treasonable son, Absalom. "Is the young man Absalom safe?" he anxiously inquired of the messenger. No, the young man was not safe; he was dead, and he had broken his father's heart!

Absalom aspired to be a king but had no kingly qualities. He lacked one thing: character. What an awful tragedy!

A few years ago all of America was stirred by the highly sensational libel suit brought by my old friend and college mate, former University of Georgia coach Wallace Butts, against the Curtis Publishing Company. Butts, who had won 140 victories in 22 seasons as Georgia's head coach and led his team to eight bowl games, was internationally famous. He was accused of having rigged the 1962 game between Georgia and Alabama.

Butts, who had won and lost many a game on the gridiron, was fighting the biggest game of his life—far more important than the three million dollars he was awarded in damages—for his reputation depended on the outcome. According to sports editor Jesse Outlar, the most dramatic moment of the eleven-day trial came when one of the leading witnesses was asked about the general character of Butts and replied, "Bad." One of Butts' attorneys is reported to have asked, "Can you imagine a worse day for any man than to be still alive and attend the funeral of his own reputation?"

It was a long, hard fight, but Butts won the verdict. Reputation is what others say you are, but character is what you really are.

I am sure that my old Mercer friend Wallace Butts would agree that there is nothing more valuable in life than character. It is worth far more than millions of dollars; in fact, there is no greater investment one can make than to invest in good character. If you lack it, you lack everything. Not to have character leads to ruin and disgrace, but to have it means to travel the highway of peace, happiness, and success. It is worth fighting for.

Recently I had the privilege of visiting a training school for girls. It is bad enough when boys get into trouble with the law, but it is sadder still for girls. One immediately senses a genuine feeling of concern for girls in trouble at the school. Though some of these girls at times may act inhuman, they are treated with kindness, and the goal is always to help them back to a better way of living.

Over the main entrance to the spacious living room of one of the homes were these words: "Character Counts." When I commented on the sign to the housemother, she replied without hesitating, "It is the *only* thing that counts."

Character is indeed the only thing that counts! It is the only thing we can take with us when this life is over. Everything else vanishes.

Wherever character is found throughout the world, it is the result of determination and endeavor. People ought to fight as hard as any coach to win the biggest game in life.

14

The Right Kind of Gossip

Through the ages the church has turned persecution into triumph. Stephen, the first Christian martyr, was stoned to death. Many times in the following years men and women gave their lives for freedom of conscience.

Stephen's death made the immediate situation worse for the early church. Its members were scattered far and wide, but God's hand turned persecution into gain. The church found then, as it has in all ages, that they who were scattered abroad went about telling others. The blood of the martyrs became seed of the church. In those days the gospel was not stamped out, but instead, preached in new parts of the country.

For some two hundred years the leaders of the Christians were branded as anarchists and atheists. To become a Christian meant probable torture or death. Christians were tied in sacks containing snakes and thrown into the sea. They were thrown to the lions or torn to pieces by ghastly instruments of death, but through it all true Christian courage and fortitude shone out. Christianity emerged strong and pure.

Those who were scattered abroad went everywhere gossiping about Christ. There are two kinds of gossip. One kind is a curse and a deadly canker. But these who were scattered abroad gossiped about Christ. It was a different kind of gossip, one impelled by love. They talked to others about Jesus because they loved him so much. They loved Jesus with such an intense love that they could not keep from telling others of him. The message burned within them, and they had to let others know about it.

This gossip about Jesus was not motivated by jealousy and hatred but by the power and love of Christ. It was not a malicious lie, but the truth. They gossiped of the one thing of which they were most certain. It was the gossip of Christ, who lived in their hearts. It came from men and women who were ready to give their very lifeblood to spread the good news of Christian faith abroad.

Is there not something for us to learn from this spontaneous action of those who were scattered abroad? We, too, can be good gossipers, and whatever happens to us, whether it be ridicule or persecution, may further the good news of the gospel of Jesus Christ.

15

In God We Trust

While others may proudly flaunt their atheism, it is simply wonderful to live in a nation that affirms its faith in God to the ends of the earth.

Over a hundred years ago a troubled minister wrote to the Secretary of the Treasury of the United States and suggested that the recognition of our undying faith should be printed in some form on the coins of our nation. "This," he wrote, "would relieve us from the ignominy of heathenism."

Upon receipt of this eloquent plea the Treasurer wrote the Director of the Mint in Philadelphia, saying, "No nation can be strong except in the strength of God, or safe except in his defense. The trust of our people should be declared in our national coins."

The Director of the Mint ordered that a motto be prepared, expressing in fewest words this national recognition. Several mottoes were tried, but in 1864 there first appeared on a United States coin, a two-cent piece, the words "In God We Trust." These immortal words symbolize the faith and righteousness that exalts a nation, and bespeak the unique and indispensable contribution the church has made to our national unity.

Many of us believe in the separation of church and state, but not in separation of God from the state or the state from God. Former President of the United States Woodrow Wilson is reported to have said once, "The sum of the whole matter is that our civilization cannot survive materially unless it is redeemed spiritually. It can be saved only by becoming permeated with the

Spirit of Christ and by being made free from the practices which spring out of that spirit."

While the Constitution of the United States forbids the Congress to make any law affecting religion, in 1780 the House of Representatives passed a rule requiring that each day's session should be opened in prayer. This rule has always been practiced by both the House and Senate, saying to the world that our nation's business is too important to attend to without seeking God's guidance and blessing. The whole superstructure of government in the United States rests upon two gigantic pillars: faith in Almighty God and belief in the dignity and worth of the individual.

When these pillars crumble and fall, the red, white, and blue of freedom and democracy will dissolve into anarchy.

16

You Can't Beat That!

Take the life lived in Christ, lift it up before the world, and like a trumpet come these words, "You can't beat that!" Whether found in the house of the Lord or in the slums, a redeemed life is a challenge to the world to produce anything like it.

Three of the most vicious of life's enemies are worry, boredom, and self-centeredness. Think of all the miserable people you know. Are these not their companions?

Christianity does away with worry. It tells us that even when worse comes to worst and the whole scheme of things collapses, nothing, absolutely nothing, can pluck us out of our Heavenly Father's care and keeping. You can't beat that!

The Christian religion also puts the finishing touches on boredom. The early disciples were often puzzled, mystified, and even frightened, but they were never bored. Never! There is never a dull moment for a Christian.

And self-centeredness! When Christ moves in, self moves out and one can say, "It is no longer I who live, but Christ who liveth in me."

Just think of it! Life's worst enemies slain and buried too deep for resurrection. You can't beat that!

One day as Josiah Royce sat in his study at Harvard University a young student asked him, "What is your definition of a Christian?" The eminent philosopher, looking out a window across the campus, replied, "I do not know how to define a Christian . . . but wait," he exclaimed, "there goes Phillips Brooks." His definition was a living one.

One of the finest monuments in America stands outside of Trinity Church in Boston, depicting this saint, Phillips Brooks, with Christ by his side, his hand resting on the preacher's shoulder, the Bible in the preacher's hands. It is said that the sculptor came to see that Phillips Brooks could not be explained apart from Jesus Christ.

Don't be misled by gloomy caricatures of Christianity. Jesus is the King of joy. Make friends with him. Look full in his wonderful face, listen to the music of his voice, and rise up and follow him into the happiest life on earth.

You can't beat it!

17

Sour Saints and Cheerful Sinners

Righteousness has not always been an admirable quality, and righteous people have not always been the most lovable people. All of us have known some sour saints and cheerful sinners and at times, no doubt, have preferred the latter.

Jesus insists upon a superior type of righteousness. The scribes were noted teachers of the Law, and the Pharisees were the most celebrated professors of it. Both groups were trained in a knowledge of the 613 traditional commands. What more could God require but strict obedience to every single one? The teachers labored hard to obey, but in their effort to be righteous they became self-righteous.

The main thesis of the Sermon on the Mount is that a Christian's righteousness must go beyond self-righteousness and mere external obedience to the Law.

"For scarcely for a righteous man will one die," said Paul, "yet peradventure for a good man some would even dare to die" (Rom. 5:7). As the apostle Paul sees him, the good man is the righteous man with an extra plus, something that makes righteousness very attractive. The good man has righteousness with love.

There is a wrong kind of righteousness, one that is hard, cold, relentless, merciless, exacting, and unsympathetic. Such righteousness does not win our love. Righteousness without love makes men bigots, narrow, harsh in judgment, intolerant, domineering, and sometimes leads them to become persecutors. It may have been upon such righteousness as this that Jesus pronounced his woes.

There is no better illustration of the wrong kind of zeal for righteousness than that which we find in Saul of Tarsus. He was a harsh, brutal, intolerant bigot when Jesus Christ laid hold of him on the road to Damascus and changed his life into something beautiful and gracious. We may be sure that there is no righteousness that is not permeated through and through with love. The righteousness which is of God is strong, compassionate, pure, loving, truthful, merciful, unswerving in fidelity, and humble and gracious.

Some time ago my car became overheated and I had to stop at the side of one of our fast expressways. Hundreds of cars went by, but I had hardly pulled off the road before a mechanic who had been right behind me came to my aid. He ran several errands for me, helped with my car, and lent me his own car to finish the journey while mine was being hauled in. Never in all my experience had I known such a good Samaritan. I thanked him profusely and asked what church he belonged to. Imagine my surprise when he said, "I do not belong to a church." No doubt hundreds of professing Christians had passed me by. As I thought of the unusual thoughtfulness and kindness of a man who did not even profess to be a Christian, I could not help but think of the words of Jesus, "Except your righteousness shall exceed . . . ye shall in no case enter into the kingdom of heaven" (Matt. 5:20).

"Not every one that saith unto me, Lord, Lord, shall enter into the kingdom of heaven; but he that doeth the will of my Father," says Jesus (7:21).

> Not he that nameth the name
> But he that doeth the will.

Our Lord plainly expects a great deal more of saints than he does of sinners.

18

Preparing for Eternity

A master sergeant in the United States Air Force was aboard a plane which had just lifted its wings and become airborne. As the plane soared, the sergeant, a fine Christian who earnestly believed in evangelism and practiced it, pulled from his pocket a little religious tract entitled, "Where Will You Spend Eternity?" He gave it to a young airman who was seated by his side.

Already a bit nervous about the flight, the young man took a quick look at the tract and, rapidly flushing, gulped out the question, "Are we going to crash?"

Unfortunately, too many people think of religion only as an emergency valve. Some think of God as a bell boy who comes running when we push a button. Many associate the basic questions of life and life everlasting only with such crises as disease, disaster, and death.

In the Sermon on the Mount Jesus teaches us that the wise person does not wait until the day of storm to prepare. He builds his house "upon a rock," and when the rain descends and the floods come and winds blow and beat upon that house, it does not fall because it is founded upon a rock.

On February 20, 1962, John Herschel Glenn, Jr., fulfilled a personal date with destiny. He blazed the space trail for the free world with a magnificent leap into orbit that carried him three times around the earth. For months upon months and years upon years he had worked unswervingly to be ready when this opportunity came. A deeply consecrated Christian, he reminded the television world shortly before his flight into space that religion should not be a thing handy only in emergencies; he told how he had always prayed and depended upon God.

If you want to find the right answers concerning where you are going to spend eternity, don't wait until you are about to crash. Seek them right now!

19

Who, Me?

An interesting advertisement appeared some time ago in a leading magazine in comic strip fashion. It carried the familiar poster of Uncle Sam with pointed finger and underneath, the words "Uncle Sam Needs You." The artist had Uncle Sam pointing toward a ten-year-old boy who asks, "Who, me?"

In the next square Uncle Sam answers, "Not right now, sonny. But you just wait! This whole great country is going to be needing you. Say about fifteen years from now when you've acquired a little algebra, and a best girl, and a 100-odd more pounds of bone and muscle."

"What'll it need me for then?" the boy asks. "For lots of things," Uncle Sam replies. The conversation continues until Uncle Sam finally says, "Yes, sonny, we're all going to need you. And all of us—father and mothers, soldiers, men and women of American industry—are working and fighting now to make sure that this world of the future will be a better world. A world in which a young man like you can find the fullest opportunities to work and build and play."

When I remember this young lad looking questioningly into the face of Uncle Sam, I think of all the young people of the world standing in the presence of Jesus Christ, looking him in the face and hearing him say, "I need you, and I need you right now, not fifteen years from now." I wonder what youth would say. Would someone ask, "Who, me?"

If so, Christ's answer is "Yes, you!" Christ needs and wants you.

He wants you to help him build a better world, not fifteen years from now, but *now*. He needs you today. He needs you to help him build better homes, schools, colleges, churches. He needs you to be a minister of the gospel, a missionary, a good Christian doctor, a nurse, schoolteacher, businessman or woman, lawyer, statesman, homemaker, mother, father, Sunday School teacher, editor, scientist, or one of perhaps a hundred or more other things. If this world is ever to be like the world it ought to be, it must have dedicated young people *today*.

Christ calls for you to dedicate your life to him and to trust him as to what to do with it. He wants you to give him everything, to let him have his way with you, and to do his will through you.

"Who, me?" you ask.

"Yes, you."

20

On the Housetop with Jesus

God works in strange and mysterious ways his wonders to perform. This was certainly true in the case of Cornelius the Gentile and Peter the Jew.

An angel appeared to Cornelius telling him to send to nearby Joppa for Peter, who would tell him what to do to serve. As Cornelius' servants neared Joppa the next day, Peter went up on the housetop to pray. He became very hungry, but while dinner was being prepared he fell asleep and had the same vision three times of a great sheet, tied at each corner, let down to earth, containing all kinds of tame and wild animals, creeping things and birds. As Peter looked at them he heard a voice saying, "Rise, Peter; kill, and eat."

But because Peter was a strict Jew, the law forbade him to eat unclean flesh. So he quite naturally replied, "Not so, Lord; for I have never eaten anything that is common or unclean." And the voice from heaven said, "What God hath cleansed, that call not thou common" (see Acts 10).

The next day when Cornelius fell upon his knees at Peter's feet, Peter put into practice what he had learned on the housetop. He said to Cornelius, a Gentile of the "Italian band," "Stand up; I myself also am a man," and added, "Ye know how that it is an unlawful thing for a man that is a Jew to keep company, or come unto one of another nation; but God hath showed me that I should not call any man common or unclean" (vv. 26, 28).

This was the best news Cornelius had ever heard. On the

housetop of Simon the tanner in Joppa, Peter had learned his lesson. God made it unmistakably clear to him that the gospel is for all people. When Peter looked into the faces of the group in Cornelius' home, he saw once again the vision of the sheet let down from heaven and he knew what it meant.

Cornelius said to Peter, "Now therefore are we all here present before God, to hear all things that are commanded thee of God" (v. 33). Peter proceeded with a message from God, saying, "Of a truth I perceive that God is no respecter of persons: but in every nation he that feareth him, and worketh righteousness, is accepted with him" (vv. 34–35). And Peter preached "peace by Jesus."

Immediately, they believed, and the Holy Spirit came upon them with great power. That very day new converts were baptized in the name of the Lord Jesus Christ. Jewish believers were greatly astonished that Gentiles, as well as Jews, could receive salvation, but they joined the Christians in praising God.

What about us? Have we ever been on the housetop with Jesus? Such an experience changes one's attitude toward those of all races.

21

Mending Shoes for Jesus

Dr. William Stidger has given us the beautiful story of Saint Anthony. He was a good man. He prayed and read his Bible for hours every day, but one day the Lord told Anthony that he was not as good as he might be. There was one other man in the world better than he. Anthony very anxiously asked the Lord to tell him who this man was. If he could only know the secret of this man's life, he would apply it to his own. The Lord told him the man was Conrad the cobbler, who lived in Jerusalem.

Bright and early one morning Saint Anthony entered Conrad's shop in Jerusalem and was cordially welcomed. Conrad inquired if he could be of service. Anthony told Conrad that he understood that he was the best man in the world and would like to know what he did to be so good. Conrad remonstrated concerning his goodness, but said, "If you wish to know what I do, I don't mind telling you. I mend shoes for a living, and I mend every pair as if I were mending them for Jesus."

Jesus says very clearly, "Whosoever will be chief among you, let him be your servant" (Matt. 21:27). The greatest in the kingdom, according to Jesus, are those who serve the most. Service is the rent we owe for the space we occupy in God's world. It is the most eloquent thing on earth.

Every person should earnestly desire to make this a better world in which to live. This is our debt to oncoming generations. What a pity to live for self when one can live for Jesus!

But no person can live for and serve Jesus who does not live for and serve others. They who live for Jesus would rather live a life than make a living, rather serve than be served. They prefer giving to receiving and losing their lives to saving them. Their prayer is:

> Help me in all the work I do
> To ever be sincere and true,
> And know that all I'd do for you
>> Must needs be done for Others.

22

Are You Ready?

The word "alert" is well known in the air force, as it doubtless is in all branches of military service. Almost everywhere I looked, on two air force bases in Newfoundland, I saw this word. Men came to worship dressed in "alert" clothing, sat in the "alert" section, and kept their eyes on the "alert" signal. At the flash of a light they were ready to dash away to duty, perhaps to crawl into a big jet or tanker and be on their way to a vital mission. Special parking places are arranged for men on alert. Men live in alert quarters around the clock. Never have I seen such alertness as I saw in the United States Air Force.

It is highly comforting, in the midst of world tension which could erupt into war, to know that Uncle Sam keeps a careful watch on the enemy and is ready for action at less than a drop of the hat. Surely we should be grateful for our nation's preparedness, not only to meet, but also to destroy the enemy, if need be.

But as important as military alertness is, it is far more important that we be spiritually alert. We must ever be watchful against sin and the devil. Hamlet is right, "Readiness is all." That great commander-in-chief of the Allied Forces during World War I, General Ferdinand Foch, said as he was dying, "I am ready."

Woodrow Wilson lived on "ready street." When asked to become president of Princeton, he said, "I am ready." When asked to become governor of New Jersey and President of the United States, he could say, "I am ready." And as he lay dying, Admiral Grayson, with tears rolling down his cheeks, pressed his hand. He seemed to say, "This is the last time; you are not far from death." Mr. Wilson seemed to understand and with a sweet smile said, "You have done all you could. The old machine is broken down. I am ready."

People do not stumble into success, nor do they just happen to get to heaven. They prepare for it. "The secret of success," said Benjamin Disraeli, once Prime Minister of England, "is for a man to be ready for his opportunity when it comes."

There are those who always have oil in their lamps and their wicks trimmed. They are eternally vigilant. Such is Phil Hays, a young airman from North Carolina, whom I met at Goose Bay. I was attracted by what appeared to be a long, miniature ladder of medals hanging on his breast. It was quite different from most of the breastwork we see on soldiers. There were sixteen rungs on the small ladder. He said he had three more at home. All of this represented nineteen years of perfect attendance at Sunday School, and he was only twenty-two. Here was a real soldier of Christ.

> My soul, be on thy guard;
>   Ten thousand foes arise;
> The hosts of sin are pressing hard
>   To draw thee from the skies.
>
> O watch and fight and pray;
>   The battle ne'er give o'er;
> Renew it boldly ev'ry day,
>   And help divine implore.

23

Roses for the Living

The day after Easter I received a beautiful letter which touched my heart deeply. It went like this:

Dear Dr. Wesberry:

I almost didn't write this note and then I remembered reading the following: "A noted editor once noticed a particularly fine achievement by a friend, also an editor. He thought he would write immediately a letter of congratulations to his friend. But he didn't. There was a day or two of delay and then he said to himself, 'Oh, pshaw! He will get hundreds of other notes about it, so I shall not bother him with mine.' Then he met his friend and told him how it happened he had failed to send his letter of commendation. 'How many do you think I did receive?' asked the friend. The editor guessed many scores, but the real answer was, 'Not one.'"

This good lady thanked me for my Easter sermon, then added, "I am sure mine will not be the only gratitude you will receive, but in any event I just had to let you know what is in my heart."

How many of us ever take time to let others know what is in our hearts? Often we intend to do so but wait until it is too late.

One day I had lunch with a man who owns over fifty-two million dollars worth of buildings. I found this multimillionaire deeply interested in people. He spoke simply and kindly. I could feel the warmth of his friendly spirit. For years I had wanted to have contact with this great man. As we talked he reached into his desk drawer and pulled out his favorite poem. It was his motto. I asked him to autograph it for me. Some of the words are:

> Around this corner I have a friend
> In this great city that has no end;
>
> . . . .
>
> "Tomorrow," I say, "I will call on Jim,
> Just to show that I'm thinking of him."
> But tomorrow comes—and tomorrow goes
> And the distance between us grows and grows.
>
> Around the corner—yet miles away—
> "Here's a telegram, sir."
>   "Jim died today."

For 994 weeks in a row every Sunday, no matter where he went, a minister received a red rose and did not know where it came from. After nineteen years he finally found out that a seventy-seven-year-old deacon had been sending them.

"A rose to the living," my friends, is indeed far "more than sumptuous wreaths to the dead."

24

Unimportant People?

An airline spokesman, speaking concerning the crack-up of a Chilean propeller-driven airliner which crashed into a mountain peak in the Andes killing sixty-seven people, was quoted in a news report as making the amazing statement that there were "no important personalities" on board.

It is most difficult to imagine anyone making such a statement. There *are* no unimportant people.

Maybe you don't think so, but you are a very important person. If you were to travel all over the world, you could never find another exactly like you; and if you could know every person who ever lived from the time of Adam until now, you wouldn't be able to discover anyone just like you.

To me this is an incredible miracle. You are a wonder of God's creation. Go look at yourself in the mirror. You are unique. There is no one in all the world just like you. God made it that way.

A verse that came out of World War I goes something like this:

My padre, he says I'm a sinner,
    And John Bull, he says I'm a saint.
But they're both of them bound to be liars,
    For I'm neither of 'em, I ain't.
I'm a man, and a man is a mixture
    Right down from the day of his birth.
Part of him comes from heaven,
    And part of him comes from earth.

The most important thing about man is that "part of him comes from heaven." That is the real man. Let us never forget it!

We ought to be grateful that we are human beings. Oh, I know, man has made an awful mess of many things on earth, and he is sometimes more like the devil than the angels. But, after all, he has done a far better job with the world than any other animal ever has, for God intended it so.

"What is man, that thou art mindful of him?" asks the psalmist. "For thou hast made him a little lower than the angels, and hast crowned him with glory and honour. Thou madest him to have dominion" (8:4–6).

Yes, dominion! God made man to have dominion, not only over all sheep, oxen, beasts of the field, fowl of the air, and fish of the sea, but also over himself and all the varied circumstances of life.

There is something good, big, fine, and noble in all of us. No matter who we are, we can do great things with our lives if we will only turn them over to God.

In his *Seven Pillars of Wisdom,* T. H. Lawrence tells how he took some Arabs from the hot deserts of Arabia and entertained them in one of the finest hotels in Paris. No matter what he attempted to show them, they were always found admiring the faucet on the bathtub. When time came for them to leave, he found them with a monkey wrench trying to detach the faucet. When he asked what they were doing they said, "We are taking the faucets off to take back to the desert." They explained that when there was no water, all they would have to do would be to take out the faucets and turn them on.

Lawrence had to explain to them that you cannot get water from a faucet unless it is connected to a water source.

So it is with our lives. They are important in God's sight, but they can never be what we or God want them to be unless they are linked through repentance, faith, and self-giving to the true source of spiritual power.

25

Championship Religion

Many people want a bargain-counter religion. There are too few of us who are ready, willing, and eager to pay the full price.

David was ready. Araunah offered him everything he needed without cost to make the sacrifice demanded of him. It was not because David was ungrateful that he refused, but because he felt the overwhelming need in his soul to make the sacrifice himself. If David had let another do it for him, he would have lost the blessing. His gift had the mark of deep sincerity.

Ananias and Sapphira were concerned only about appearances. Desiring the esteem of those who gave their all, they claimed that they also had when they hadn't.

Almost everything worth having in life is costly.

This is true in championship athletics. The great football games played on New Year's Day seem so easy to many spectators, but, oh! what a price the men have to pay in years of self-denial, regular training, drill after drill, and often injury after injury.

What about championship education? No person can become educated who is unwilling to pay the price of determination and willingness to study.

Nor does a happy home just happen. Successful homes are built by husbands and wives who are willing to pay the cost in thought, prayer, and action. A championship home costs something almost every minute of every hour.

Businessmen know too that the championship workman, who-ever he is, often toils while others sleep. Places of excellence are never won on cheap terms but always at the cost of energy, discipline, self-control, and the utmost giving of self.

There are no real accomplishments without cost. The costliest thing on earth, though, is religion. Think of what it cost God—it cost him everything! If our gifts reveal the quality of our love, then what about God's? He gave his Son for us. Jesus left his home in heaven to dwell among us. "He came unto his own, and his own received him not" (John 1:12). He told his disciples that he must go to Jerusalem and suffer, and when Peter argued, Jesus said, "It is going to cost me." And it did. "His sweat was as it were great drops of blood falling down to the ground" (Luke 22:44). The cross tells us how much he paid for our redemption.

What is our response? We can turn Christ's grief into joy. He offers us a share in his costly kingdom enterprise, but he offers no man a cheap, easy-going religion. A comfortable religion is a bad religion.

Lenin said, "For revolution, I must have a man or woman prepared to shun delights and live laborious days."

This, my friends, is true of the kingdom of God.

The application of the principle of this text will transform our lives. But we must be willing to say, "I will not offer unto the Lord my God that which cost me nothing."

26

The Language of Sympathy

Tears are the language of sympathy in all nations. Everybody understands the language of tears.

Many years ago Woodrow Wilson's secretary came into his private office to find him weeping as though his heart would break. "Why the tears, Mr. Wilson?" he asked.

"I am weeping," he replied, "for the imperiled liberties of the world."

The shortest verse in the Bible tells us that "Jesus wept." The creator of this world, in whom all things consist, the author of our salvation, the great head of our churches, the King of kings and Lord of lords, wept.

He foretold his own tragic death. He saw the dark, unspeakable sorrow of Gethsemane ahead, the cruel crown of thorns, and the rusty nails, but he never wept for himself. His were tears of sympathy at a time of sorrow. His friend Lazarus was dead. Others were weeping and so was he. Such tears speak louder than words to our hearts.

How wonderful it is to see him speak to the raging billows and know that they obey him; to see him touch a blind man's eyes and know that he goes away seeing; to hear him speak to a paralytic and see the once lame man carry his bed away; to see him cleanse ten lepers, though only one returned to thank him. How marvelous to witness Jesus' healing powers. But when Jesus goes with us to the graveside where our beloved are buried, and stands in our midst with a tear-stained face and a sobbing heart, how real he is to us and how we love him!

A tomb without Jesus is a sad, gloomy, lonely place, afflicting the heart with melancholy and despair. What a difference it makes when Jesus stands there! Hope, love, and immortality combine in him.

When you are called upon to visit the grave of a loved one or to go to a new grave, ask the Saviour to go with you. Then you will not seek among the dead those who live forever and are clothed with immortality. Your heart will not be filled with sadness, but with joy unspeakable, glorious.

For if Jesus stands with you at the tomb of your loved one, you will see the dawn of an eternal day and you will hear his sweet voice saying, "The hour is coming, and now is, when the dead shall hear the voice of the Son of God: and they that hear shall live" (John 5:25).

27

O for a Bigger Boat!

One hot summer day a small party of us walked the Via Dolorosa in Jerusalem and turned aside to visit the pool of Bethesda. Written on the walls nearby in 135 languages is the lovely story of Bethesda, which means "The House of Mercy." The "house of mercy" was really a house of misery, ignorance, superstition, dirt, filth, poverty, disease, rags, and suffering. There was a tradition there that occasionally an angel entered into the pool and troubled the water. The people believed that when the water bubbled, the first man to step into it would be healed of whatever disease he might have. At such times everyone made a desperate rush for the pool. It was a pitiful sight.

One of the men there had been crippled for thirty-eight years. He had no family or friends. Others had somehow managed to get into the pool when the water was troubled, but not he. He had waited over a third of a century. It all seemed so hopeless. The only explanation he could give was, "When the water is troubled I have no man to put me in."

One day Jesus came to Bethesda and his eyes fell on this poor crippled man. "Wilt thou be made whole?" he asked.

"Sir, I have no man, when the water is troubled, to put me into the pool: but while I am coming, another steppeth down before me." The Master of all mercy and kindness said, "Rise, take up thy bed, and walk" (see John 5:1–8).

The story of the angel troubling the water is mere legend, but Jesus is real. He spent his life lifting up those who had been knocked down, speaking kind words to those who were hurt, healing and setting upon their feet those who were crippled. In the place of misery Christ built the house of mercy.

How we do need to see human need through the eyes of Jesus! When Jesus saw the multitudes, he had compassion on them. There are multiplied thousands of people all around us, who, when the water is troubled, have no one to put them into the pool. They need your help. As God sent Christ to build houses of mercy, so Christ sends us.

We are told that many years ago two boats, the Princess Alice and the Bywell Castle, collided at sea. Six hundred of the nine hundred excursionists perished in the dense fog. That same night two ferrymen were mooring their boats. One heard the crash and said, "I am tired and I am going home; no one will see me in the fog." The other did all he could to help. Both ferrymen were called to appear at the coroner's inquest. When the first man was asked, "Did you hear the cries?" he replied, "Yes, sir."

"What did you do?" inquired the coroner.

"Nothing, sir," he answered sadly.

"Are you an Englishman?" the coroner asked.

"Yes, sir," he confirmed.

"Aren't you ashamed of yourself?" rebuked the coroner.

"Sir," he groaned, "the shame will never leave me till I die."

Of the other the coroner asked, "And what did you do?" The second man replied, "I jumped into the boat and pulled for the wreck with all my might; I crammed my boat with women and children, and when it was too dangerous to take even one other, I rowed with the cry, 'O Lord, for a bigger boat!'"

If we fail to do our best for those who cry for help all about us, the shame will never leave us until we die.

O Lord, for a bigger boat!

28

Sunrise, Not Sunset

Few things are more beautiful or stunning than a golden sunset. It is easy to see why the poet describes death as "sunset," "evening star," "twilight," "evening bell," and "the dark." One of our most beloved hymns expresses the same idea:

> Abide with me, fast falls the eventide,
> The darkness deepens, Lord with me abide.

As beautiful as it is to think of death as sunset, Easter reminds us that death is not sunset, but sunrise. The sunset is but a reflection of a far vaster beauty, for it is but the cloud-reflected light from the hidden sun. While from our view it may appear as sunset, it is sunrise beyond the setting sun elsewhere. Thus the beauty of the sunset is a revelation of the greater life of the unseen sun, shining more radiantly on another shore. As Clement of Alexandria once said, "Christ has turned our sunsets into sunrise."

Death for a Christian is sunrise, not sunset; it is not death, but dawn; not darkness, but light; not gloom, but glory; not the end of day, but daybreak; not sundown, but sunup; not our last great enemy, but our friend; not an end, but a beginning; not an exit, but an entrance; not an annihilation, but everlasting life; not dust, but durability. We are not as rubbish cast "to the void," but we are "transplanted human worth that blooms to profit otherwhere."

Death is not, as Shelley says, "lying down on the lone couch of everlasting sleep," but it is rising up to walk all over God's heaven. Death is not an eternal sleep. "There is no death; what seems so is transition."

The first Easter dawned upon death. The last word on Good Friday was death, death, death. Despair, shame, and fear gripped the disciples. But we read, "They went to the tomb when the sun had risen."

After Easter the last word is life, life, *life*. Easter changed shame to glory, fear to faith, despair to gladness, sunset to sunrise.

> Sunrise tomorrow, sunrise tomorrow,
>> Sunrise in glory is waiting for me;
> Sunrise tomorrow, sunrise tomorrow,
>> Sunrise with Jesus for eternity.

29

When Self Sticks Out

One day one of the world's greatest surgeons, Dr. Charles Mayo, came into a room dragging one of his legs. When someone inquired about it, Dr. Mayo replied: "There is a passage in the Bible which says, 'They made me a keeper of the vineyards; but mine own vineyard have I not kept.' I saw this coming on but I would not pay it heed." He had failed to take seriously the advice he gave to others.

Many people drag themselves lamely through life because they will not discipline themselves to the best they know. The lack of discipline strikes back in impoverished minds, bodies, and souls. One of life's spiritual laws is that you are either disciplined or you become decadent.

Just as the climb to physical fitness is not easy, so neither is the climb to spiritual fitness. Miss America of 1945, addressing a group of high school students, said, "You cannot hate and be beautiful." Hate is undisciplined love. No person can be undisciplined and be really beautiful.

One of the greatest paintings in all the world is *The Last Supper* by Leonardo da Vinci, which took him three years to complete. He painted it on the wall of a convent refectory long ago in Florence, Italy. One of the most unusual things about this painting is that each character was drawn from real life, the figures being one and a half times life-size. The artist made individual studies of each of the characters and sought to portray exactly what he thought would be their specific reaction to Christ's announcement, "One of you shall betray me."

The story is told that during the painting of this picture he had a bitter argument with another artist and sought vengeance by painting his face as Judas Iscariot. When at last he came to paint the face of Jesus Christ he tried and tried, but could not satisfy himself. Everything seemed to go wrong. Plagued by feelings of guilt and shame he finally sponged out the face of Judas Iscariot, and that night in a dream he saw the image of the Lord which later he painted. There was the picture he had longed to paint which he could not until he removed all bitterness from his heart.

We are all painting a picture with our own lives, but it can never be done satisfactorily until we get rid of all selfishness, resentment, and bitterness.

The great poet Tennyson says:

Love
Smote the chords of self, which trembling,
Passed in music out of sight.

You cannot have an unclean mind if your heart is pure. The place to begin discipline is in our hearts. The trouble with most of us is that self sticks out. I am reminded of a woman who, having been miraculously healed from paralysis, prayed, "Now, Lord, you've healed me, what are you going to do about my overweight?"

The first thing to give up is self. When self is on the throne, Christ is on the cross, but when self climbs down from the throne and goes to the cross, Christ becomes enthroned in our hearts.

30

Strength for Life's Roughness

Extending from the wings of the great, powerful 707 Boeing jets is a series of blades known as vortex generators. Their purpose is to roughen the air when the weather is smooth. They cause the air to swirl toward the rear section of the plane, giving enough turbulence for accurate steering.

Imagine that! The designer of this plane found it necessary to create roughness to enable the plane to hold its direction and to reach its destination safely.

Could it also be true that the supreme Architect of the universe placed generators on the path of our lives to help us develop the right sense of direction and fulfil his destiny for our lives? Is roughness along life's way a part of God's plan?

The psalmist thought so. "It is good for me," he said, "to have been in trouble." The great apostle Paul tells that everything that happened to him was for the furtherance of the gospel.

If we have no problems, we might well ask the good Lord to give us some. Problems are a sign of life and the more problems we have, the more life we have. There are no problems in the city of the dead.

God knows that our lives will never be what they ought to be without difficulties. He wants us to be strong, courageous, stalwart men and women. He allows us to have problems in order to test and develop our character and to help us grow bigger and more Christlike souls.

The people who live nearest to the heart of God are always the ones who do the best with the tough situations of life. Paul could say, "I can do all things through Christ which strengtheneth me." The psalmist said, "God is our refuge and strength, a very present help in trouble" (46:1).

Many people have found the solution to all their problems in Jesus Christ. By accepting him as their Lord and Saviour and letting him come into their lives they have found power to rise above all of the problems and difficulties of life.

When someone once asked Dwight L. Moody who it was that gave him the most trouble, he replied, "That's easy. It's Dwight L. Moody." Isn't that true of us all?

Our biggest problem is the problem of self. Solve that problem and we solve all problems. When we surrender our all to Jesus Christ and let him come into our hearts it is no longer "I," but "Christ who liveth in me." Life is not our own, but his; what happens to us happens to him; and we no longer live in our own strength, but in his.

The same great God who allows the roughness along life's way also gives us strength to complete the journey.

31

The Final Proof of Greatness

The South African puff adder is one of the deadliest snakes on earth. After cleaning several snake cages of Salt Lake City's Hogle Zoo, Director Gerald de Bary opened the adder's cage. Suddenly he felt faint and reached out his left arm to keep from falling into the cage; but faster than the eye could see the adder struck at the open door, burying its fangs in de Bary's forearm. As he died, twelve hours after having been struck, de Bary said, "Don't blame the snake; it's not his fault."

There are not many people who would take such a position. It is so easy for us when we are bitten, hurt, wounded, maligned, criticized, or insulted, not only to be bitter about it, but also to fight back.

A Canadian-born Christian missionary to Israel, William L. Hull, wrestled with the spirit of genocidist Adolf Eichmann in his death cell in Jerusalem's Ramleh Prison. Out of the experience came a book by Hull entitled *The Struggle for a Soul*. He says in this book that "when the order came, Eichmann simply turned to stone. He died with great bitterness, quite unrepentant." How tragic his heinous crime and how sad his attitude!

One of the finest statements I have ever read was made by Coach Johnny Leonard Griffith of the University of Georgia who, when he was fired, said: "I have made some mistakes, but I do have the satisfaction of knowing that I always did the best for Georgia to the best of my ability. Certainly I am disappointed, *but I am not bitter.*"

Some time ago I ran across a beautiful quotation from Elbert Hubbard in *Think* magazine that I have been looking for for years. It expresses a feeling I have never been able to express as he does. It is indeed a gem of precious truth. "The man who is anybody," Hubbard says, "and who does anything is surely going to be criticized, vilified, and misunderstood. This is a part of the penalty for greatness, and every great man understands it, too, that it is no proof of greatness. The final proof of greatness lies in being able to endure contumely without resentment."

What do you do when someone mistreats you? What happens inside of you? How you react to criticism is the acid test which tells how big or little you are. It is indeed one of the distinguishing marks of a mature Christian to turn the other cheek when smitten. It isn't easy to keep bitterness out of our souls, but it is possible.

Writing in his Washington column, Drew Pearson said in an article entitled "The Greatest Tribute to JFK": "The greatest monument the American people can erect to John F. Kennedy is a spiritual monument—the eradication of hate."

Better still, let us erect a spiritual monument to Jesus Christ, who centuries ago set the supreme example of love when he prayed for his enemies, "Father, forgive them; for they know not what they do" (Luke 23:34). In this prayer he put into practice what he preached while living on earth, "Love your enemies, bless them that curse you, do good to them that hate you, and pray for them which despitefully use you, and persecute you" (Matt. 5:44).

32

Where Are the Goal Posts?

A university professor was urging a group of young men on one occasion to play the game of life well, when one of them exclaimed, "How can we play the game of life when we don't know where the goal posts are?"

Many football fans will never forget an event that took place in the Rose Bowl Game of 1929 between the University of California and Georgia Tech. The California center, Roy Riegals, received a fumble on Tech's thirty-three-yard line and ran toward the wrong goal, seventy yards away. One of his own teammates finally tackled him on the one-foot line. As Riegals realized his awful mistake, an agonized expression spread over his face. Fortunately, California's attempt to kick from behind the goal was blocked and Tech scored a safety which brought victory. The final score was Tech—8, California—7.

What a terrible tragedy that many are pursuing the wrong goals in life! They wander aimlessly with no great purpose to challenge and no great ideal to inspire them. They do not know where the goal posts are. For all who devote their efforts to the pursuit of the wrong goals and completely ignore moral objectives and spiritual aims, there is coming some day, as with Roy Riegals, a rude awakening. How ashamed all people should be who are devoting their lives to the wrong causes and running away from God!

Paul knew where the real goal posts of life were and he could say: "I press toward the mark for the prize of the high calling of God in Christ Jesus" (Phil. 3:14). Any man can carry the ball straight toward the right goal post in life if he will.

Mrs. Theresa Capone was buried a little over a decade ago by the side of her notorious son, Scarface Al. She had five sons but the world knew only four. One named Ralph was known as "Bottles." Matt was called "Mimi." Salvadore was known as "Frank." These three, along with Al, were all gangsters. But there was another Capone, a brother named James. Ashamed of his four gangster brothers and even of his name, James called himself "Harte" and went to Nebraska and became a law enforcement officer. He was so stern that lawbreakers called him "Two-gun Harte," and he was named a district commissioner of the Boy Scouts of America.

What a story! James carried the ball against great odds, and his victory was only the greater.

Christie Benet was the center for our high school football team of 1924. There was no finer young man in high school. A model student and ideal sportsman, he was president of our student body, as well as star of the team. He always played the game as if God were watching and he was playing for him. As a result of an injury received in football he died in his youth, but before he did he was heard to say, "I don't mind dying." He could say this because, like the apostle Paul, he had found out where the true goal posts of life were and was carrying the ball in that direction.

> For when the one great scorer
>   Comes to write against your name—
> He marks—not what you won or lost,
>   But how you played the game.

33

How to Improve the Church

We are living in a fault-finding age. On every hand we find people criticizing the church. Both the secular and religious press tell us what is wrong with it. Even some ministers of the gospel are complaining. The church is their favorite whipping boy.

Some of these caustic critics have the astonishing faculty of putting everyone in their place but themselves. Evidently they feel they are beyond criticism.

F. R. Barry has said, "The one really formidable argument against the truth of the Christian religion is the record of the Christian Church. Again and again it has denied its Lord, distorted his teachings, betrayed his spirit. Again and again it has taken the wrong side."

What is the church? Jesus spoke of it as "my church." Surely it is his, not ours. Christ and his church are inseparable. The church is the community of the redeemed, "the body of Christ." As such it is a Christocentric community—a divine-human institution.

As long as the church is composed of human beings, how can it be perfect? The church is made up of sinners who have been saved by grace through faith in the Lord Jesus Christ. The church is not infallible, only Christ is. If only perfect people could belong to it, then there would be no room in it for you or me.

Let me humbly acknowledge our own imperfections and agree that the church, both on the pages of history and in our generation has made mistakes. But let us also consider this question: How much good do we accomplish by always harping on the failure of the church? Isn't there anything good we can say for the church? Isn't anything right with it?

There is another side! Albert Einstein once saw it. He said: "Being a lover of freedom, when the revolution [against Nazism] came in Germany, I looked to the universities to defend it but the universities were immediately silenced. Then I looked to the editors of the newspapers whose flaming editorials in days gone by had proclaimed their love of freedom but they, like the universities, were silenced in a few short weeks. Only the Church stood squarely across the path of Hitler's campaigning for suppressing the truth. I never had any special interest in the Church before but now I feel a great affection and admiration for it because the Church alone had the courage and persistence to stand for truth and freedom. What I once despised I now praise unreservedly."

If you are one of those people who are forever finding something wrong with the church, what about taking a look at the other side and seeing if there isn't something you can "praise unreservedly"? While you ask yourself, "Is there anything right with the church?" why not also ask, "What kind of church would my church be if every member were exactly like I am?"

> I love Thy church, O God!
>> Her walls before Thee stand,
> Dear as the apple of Thine eye,
>> And graven on Thy hand.

34

Don't Miss the Damascus Road!

We are living in the greatest road-building age in human history. Roads are being built the world over. Only the ocean stops them.

As valuable and important as these great arteries are over which the vast traffic of our modern civilization circulates, there are some roads mentioned in the Bible of far greater value and importance.

There is the *Damascus road,* the road of spiritual awakening. Saul of Tarsus traveled it long ago. At the time he was the bitter enemy of the Christian way, but as he neared Damascus on that road something dramatic happened to him. He was struck down by a sudden light from heaven. For three days he was without sight, food, or drink. His experience on the Damascus road as he came face to face with Christ was the turning point of his life. He received his sight, was baptized, and "straightway he preached Christ in the synagogues, that he is the Son of God" (Acts 9:20).

This is what it means to be born again. Sometimes it comes suddenly and dramatically as in Saul's case, but more often it may be less sudden and dramatic. The important thing is that when it comes, life is changed.

Human service follows Christian experience. Thus the *Jericho road* leads off of the Damascus road. No person can be truly religious and be indifferent to human suffering. Jesus tells us of "a certain man who went from Jerusalem to Jericho, and fell among thieves." They said, "What's his is ours and we will take it." They beat him and left him nearly dead by the side of the road. A priest came and saw him but passed by on the other side, and a Levite came and looked on him and passed by. They said, "What's mine is my own and I am going to keep it."

Then came the good Samaritan. As he drew near the poor wounded man, he had compassion on him, bound up his wounds, set him on a beast, brought him to an inn, took care of and provided for him. He said, "What's mine is yours, and I am going to share it."

Often the road to Jericho leads to the *Via Dolorosa,* the road of suffering. It is the way of the cross. Jesus said, "If any man will come after me, let him deny himself, and take up his cross, and follow me (Matt. 16:24). Following Jesus in helping to make this a better world may involve pain, but whatever the cost the inner man grows and becomes more like his Lord.

The loveliest road of all is the *road to Emmaus.* The afternoon of the resurrection two tired, bewildered disciples walked this road and talked of the things that had happened in Jerusalem. Jesus himself drew near and went with them. They did not recognize him. "He expounded unto them in all the scriptures the things concerning himself" (Luke 24:27). As they came to Emmaus they invited him to dine with them, and as he blessed the bread their eyes were opened and they knew him. He vanished, and they said one to another, "Did not our hearts burn within us, while he talked with us by the way, and while he opened to us the scriptures?"

What a joyful reward! Jesus always joins his disciples as they walk the various roads of life, but he cannot do so unless they have first traveled the Damascus road.

Don't miss the Damascus road!

35

There Is Yet Hope

Many people fear that our nation has already begun to decline. They see a fatal malady in our midst and fear for the future. All who see these signs of inner decay are not fools and fanatics. Some of them are loyal patriots who love America and would gladly die for it if need be.

Underneath the proud façade of military power, economic wealth, scientific genius, industrial might, and widespread extravagance, they see ominous cracks in our nation's foundation. Like the Hebrew prophets of old they insist that, as in the past, national corruption precedes national collapse and that continued greatness depends on the degree to which we apply the teachings of God's Holy Word to our individual, national, and social lives.

A short time ago I visited Iraq—old Mesopotamia—the land between the great Tigris and Euphrates rivers where the Garden of Eden is supposed to have been. It is the country of Abraham, Daniel, and Nebuchadnezzar. While in Baghdad I took a side trip to ancient Babylon. With all of its past glory, majestic palaces, temples, hanging gardens, and beautiful homes, clothing, and jewelry, it appears as a mess of old, dusty-looking bricks today, buried in the sands of time and forgotten except for its name, printed on a sign.

The ruins of ancient Babylon preach a powerful sermon. Arnold Toynbee, one of the world's foremost historians, lists in his *Study of History* nineteen great civilizations that have collapsed, only three of which have been conquered by enemies from without. The other sixteen gave way because of weaknesses within, such as idleness, drunkenness, and immorality.

On top of this that great world historian, Edward Gibbon, sets forth in *The Decline and Fall of the Roman Empire* the basic reasons for the catastrophic collapse of the mighty Roman empire: the rapid increase of divorce; the undermining of the dignity and sanctity of the home, the foundation of civilization; higher and higher taxes; the spending of public money for free bread and circuses for the people; the mad craze for pleasure; the development every year of more exciting, more brutal, more immoral sports; the building of great armaments while individual responsibility diminished; and the decay of religion.

If these are signs of approaching national collapse, what do we see when we apply them to our own nation? Are not these same termites eating into the timbers of our own foundations? How long will it take us to learn the lessons of history? The prophets of old warned Israel repeatedly of their impending doom if they did not forsake their wicked and idolatrous ways and worship the living God. Have not all captivities come as the result of forgetting God? Has any civilization ever fallen where its people were right with God?

It is late, but not too late, for God says: "If my people, which are called by my name, shall humble themselves, and pray, and seek my face, and turn from their wicked ways; then will I hear from heaven, and will forgive their sin, and will heal their land" (2 Chron. 7:14).

36

Between the Hamburgers and God

A patient explained to his doctor that he was very tired. After a thorough examination the good physician told him that one reason for his depletion of energy was that his blood sugar was low. The man naturally thought the doctor would prescribe sweets, but to his surprise the doctor told him to eat hamburger every day for lunch.

"It is not only your blood sugar that is down," added the doctor. "Your spiritual life is depleted. When you build that up your blood sugar will be better. I prescribe that you go to church Sunday after Sunday and expose yourself to the atmosphere of the place; let it wash your mind, and find God again. Between the hamburgers and God," he concluded, "you will be a well man again."

It has probably never occurred to many of us that religion affects our bodies as well as our minds. Tiredness comes from physical exertion, structural disease, or old age. If after a good night's rest we are still tired, our trouble may be mental and spiritual.

There are many emotions that sap our energy. Nothing drains us more than feelings of guilt. Resentment depletes us. If we hate, hate destroys us. Worries, fears, self-centeredness, boredom, indecision, and over-sensitivity—each takes its toll. No amount of rest can rest a sinner until he rests his soul in God.

Some time ago I was called to a home of sorrow. After years of sickness, death had come to a loved one. The gracious wife had been more than faithful. She had stood by and cared for her husband when such strength should have been impossible.

As I talked to her about her husband's funeral, I asked what her favorite Scripture verse was. Without a moment's hesitation she replied, "I'd like for you to use Isaiah 40:31." When I turned to the passage in my Bible I found the familiar words beautiful, comforting, and strengthening: "They that wait upon the Lord shall renew their strength; they shall mount up with wings as eagles; they shall run, and not be weary; and they shall walk, and not faint."

Couple with this the words of Jesus in Matthew 12:28-30, and we have God's answer to our tiredness: "Come unto me, all ye that labour and are heavy laden, and I will give you rest. Take my yoke upon you . . . . For my yoke is easy, and my burden is light."

George Gallup asked 402 people in all parts of the country who were over ninety-five and still in good health how they got so far in such good shape. He found that diet and a pleasant frame of mind were important factors, and that 97 percent of these people were religious. He concluded that if you want to live a short life, you should smoke a lot, drink a lot, complain a lot, worry a lot, and stay away from church.

If we really want the restoration of life's vitality, energy, enthusiasm, and power, we must turn everything in our lives over to God and trust in him. There is more re-creative power in Christianity than in all the drugstores and health resorts of the world.

You cannot ignore religion if you want healthy minds and bodies.

37

The Only Way Out of the Dark

Blind Helen Keller once said, "Truly the Bible, the teaching of our Savior, is the only way out of the dark."

The Bible is more than any man or all men have ever said of it. It is the record of the progressive revelation of God through the religious experiences of his chosen people. As such, it is a miraculous, supernatural revelation. The Bible is the world's greatest book and earth's best seller.

In spite of all this, it is often buried beneath other books or papers, pushed into a remote corner, or given a place where spiders spin their webs. Consequently, there is an appalling, widespread ignorance of its contents.

When a little girl was asked if she knew anything that was in the Bible, her answer was shocking and revealing. "Yes," she said, "there's a pressed squirrel tail, a rose from Aunt Molley's grave, a lock of Grandpa's hair, an insurance receipt, and Pa's Masonic emblem."

On a simple Bible test given to 99 high school students, 44 did not know who Joseph was, 51 would not place Luke, 46 did not know who Herod and Pilate were, 60 did not know the name of the mother of Jesus, 10 did not know where Christ was born, 5 did not know the opening phrase of the Lord's Prayer, and 90 did not know where to find the Ten Commandments.

College students didn't do any better. Out of 281, all but 12 of which had attended Sunday school regularly, 222 failed to identify Matthew as the tax collector who became a disciple; 208 could not recall who the father of Joseph and his brothers was; 197 did not know what book the Ten Commandments are in; 183 could not recognize Solomon as the famous wise man of the Old Testament; and 169 did not know a single parable of Jesus.

A soldier during World War II was hit above the heart by a small shell. He carried a small New Testament in his shirt pocket. The shell struck the Testament and the soldier lived. He exclaimed, "I will never go anywhere again without a Bible; it saved my life."

Many a person can say, "The Bible saved my life," because instead of carrying in in their pockets, as fine as that is, they hide its teachings in their hearts. It points them to the One who saves. On every page there is light, love, and life.

Dwight L. Moody once said, "Sin will keep you from this book, but this book will keep you from sin."

It is time for us to turn once again to our Bibles. How long will it take us to learn that many of the tragedies in our lives, homes, and nation today are due to our neglect of God's Word? The Bible is God's book, and it is yours if you will accept it.

Read it as never before. It will lead you out of the dark. It will make you wise above your fellows, wise even unto salvation.

> Let all the plans that men devise
>> Assault that book with treacherous art;
> I'll call them vanity and lies,
>> And bind that Bible to my heart.

38

Let the Church Be the Church

Some years ago Dean Samuel Miller of Harvard Divinity School was quoted in a magazine article as saying, "The church has become almost as monastic as the orders in the Middle Ages. There seems to be no connection between what happens in the church and what happens in society, except that people living in a desperate age use it to tranquilize their disturbing experiences like some kind of lullaby."

Have our churches failed? Some outstanding churchmen assert that in many ways they have. One thing to which we will all agree is that many of us have failed as church members. No church is ever stronger or better than its individual members.

Some people seem to think that if the church is not doing what the government or the press is doing, it is doing nothing. We repudiate this idea. We do not expect the government to preach the love and forgiveness of the cross and neglect the business of the state. Neither do we expect the church to have as its primary function the security and well-being of the state.

While our churches cannot assume full responsibility in all of the decisions of our day, we may well hope and pray that in the political, military, economic, and intellectual world men and women may think the thoughts of Christ and seek above everything else to do his will.

The main function of the church is to lift the cross high above every principality and power. The cross humbles, mellows, subdues, and causes us to realize our lustfulness, greediness, pride, intolerance, rebellion, and impenitence. God forbid it, but if the whole world should some day be destroyed, let at least the name of Jesus Christ stand above every name and the cross of Christ shine above every symbol.

The church must remain absolutely faithful to her Lord, guarding the divine mysteries entrusted to her. Let her wield the weapons of God's Holy Spirit in the face of anti-truth, untruth, sin, and error by strongly maintaining the right order of value; by declaring that the Spirit comes first and everything else second; and by affirming God as Creator, Christ as Savior, and the Holy Spirit as the giver of life and guide into all truth. The church must weigh all economic, social, and political questions in the light of the mind of Christ and be free to preach the gospel all over the world. The big business of the church is to win the lost to Christ, to instil the love and fear of God in human hearts, to fight the devil, live wholly by faith, and seek unity among all who name the name of Christ.

Such a church never fears failure. As Jesus said, "The gates of hell shall not prevail against it" (Matt. 16:18).

Let the church be the church!

39

Let Us Live Before We Die

The greatest aristocracy in all the world is the aristocracy of service. This aristocracy is composed of those who would rather live a life than make a living. They have no thought of themselves. They want no reward or recognition. All they want is to serve.

What a tragedy it is to live a useless, purposeless life! How we pity the people who live only for themselves when they could be living for others.

How shall we ever forget the day when Dr. Theron Rankin, missionary then for over twenty years in China, came to one of our conventions in South Carolina, having just returned from six months in a Japanese prison camp? He was weak and emaciated and very thin. As he ascended the stairs which led to the pulpit, that great convention stood to its feet in silent appreciation of one who had really given himself in the Master's service. Yes, the world bows down to the man who serves it.

How beautiful and inspiring is unselfish service for Christ. Some years ago a lovely lady in Atlanta was recognized as Atlanta's Woman of the Year in Civic Affairs. Her service was said to have been unmatched by any other woman during that year. When given a chance to speak, she said, "If I have served, I am thankful for the privilege of serving. Some people have asked me why I put so much time in civic work, and I will let you in on a secret. Years ago I decided I did not want to die without having lived, that I wanted to give myself, in a small way, to help others. I have received real enjoyment in giving myself. God has been good."

What a decision! "I decided I did not want to die without having lived." Let us be as wise, and live before we die.

> If I can stop one heart from breaking,
>   I shall not live in vain:
> If I can ease one life the aching,
>   Or cool one pain,
> or help one fainting robin
>   Unto his nest again,
>   I shall not live in vain.
>
> EMILY DICKINSON

40

Regaining What We Have Lost

She was a beautiful young woman in her early twenties. She had already been married twice and both marriages had left her with a broken heart. She was disappointed and had lost faith in almost everybody. Her life had already been deeply troubled, yet from the standpoint of age she was only on life's threshold.

She took her tragic story from one responsible person to another. They all pointed her to someone else. "So what?" they seemed to say to her. "Why don't you just forget it all?" The fact that nobody seemed to care added to her hurt.

She had been wronged. Her soul was wounded. She wanted to do something about it to help others avoid the same mistakes, but nobody seemed to care.

Great big tears rolled down her cheeks as she said, "I would give anything in the world if I could only have back what I have lost. I once sang in a choir of a great church, and even taught a Sunday School class. I do not have the ideals I once had. Oh, so much has gone out of my life, and how I miss it! If I could only have it back again."

Is it possible to regain what we have lost? Can a person move backwards? Checker players don't think so. Neither did Huxley, who once said, "The unseen opponent in the great game of life, while scrupulously fair, will allow no back moves, and makes us pay in full for every blunder."

But the woman taken in adultery, Zaccheus, blundering Peter, Mary Magdalene, the woman of Samaria, and others of the New

Testament all tell us that there is a wonderful place called "the land of beginning again."

Many years ago a broken-hearted minister who had just lost his wife listened to an eminent New York preacher on the radio. Thinking that perhaps he was a man who could help, he phoned, made an appointment, and spent an hour in the pastor's study. As he was leaving, the pastor's secretary heard him exclaim, "When I went in there all the stars had been blotted out of the heavens for me, and he put them back again." As Joel of old declared, "The Lord will do great things. . . . [He] will restore to you the years that the locust hath eaten" (2:21–25).

Yes, there is one who can restore all that we have lost. He can put every star that has been blacked out of our lives back into the heavens.

Call the roll of your sins. Bring them to the foot of the cross. Christ died for them all, and he lives. His outpoured life may be poured into yours by your repentance and faith, and you may become a new creature in Christ. Why not put your trust in him?

41

Epitaph: Died of Worry

On many a tombstone it might be written, "Died of Worry."

More people worry than work themselves to death. Worry is death's best friend. Not only may it reduce the number of our years, but it also may cause us to die many deaths. It is like the constant drip, drip, drip of water. This consistent drip, drip, drip often drives people to insanity and to suicide.

Someone once said:

> I've joined the new don't worry club,
>   And now I hold my breath;
> I'm so afraid I'll worry
>   That I'm worried most to death.

But I bring you good news. You do not have to worry yourself to death. Jesus says, "Therefore, I tell you, do not worry about life. Do not wonder what you will have to eat or drink, or about your body, what you will wear" (see Matt. 6:25). Jesus assures us that we need not worry ourselves to death.

He teaches us that our heavenly Father cares for us. We are of great value to God. It displeases him for us to worry; it shows our lack of trust. Such lack of trust is sinful. "Behold the fowls of the air," said Jesus, "for they sow not, neither do they reap, nor gather into barns; yet your heavenly Father feedeth them. Are ye not much better [of more value] than they? Consider the lilies of the field . . . they toil not, neither do they spin: and yet . . . Solomon in all his glory was not arrayed like one of these. . . . If God so clothe the grass of the field, which to day is, and to morrow is cast into the oven, shall he not much more clothe you, O ye of little faith?" (Matt. 6:26–30)

Faith is the word! Let's underscore it. What Jesus means is this: "You would not worry about all these things if you had more faith. You evidently don't really know your heavenly Father. If you really knew him, you wouldn't worry so. Your heavenly Father knows that you have need of all these things. He loves you. He is able. He will supply all your needs according to his riches in glory through Jesus Christ. What about trusting him?"

"After all these things"—earthly security, comfort, pleasure, fame, wealth, honor—"do the Gentiles seek," said Jesus. "But seek ye first the kingdom of God, and his righteousness; and all these things shall be added unto you" (vv. 32–33). Put the kingdom first! Consecrate yourself to him! Lose yourself in seeking God's kingdom and righteousness and worry will vanish, and all "these things" shall be added unto you.

Worry robs us of the best there is in life and hastens death. Faith brings life and life victorious. May we be able to say, "I believe in God with all of my heart. He is my Father. There never was such a good Father as he or ever one so kind. Because he is my Father and because he is so good he will never let me perish. I will put my trust in him."

42

God's Precious Promises

Many years ago a diamond was found in South Africa worth millions of dollars. It weighed a pound and a half. It was presented to King Edward VII. Men were appointed to guard it by day and night. It was worth so much more than any diamond ever discovered that there was no standard by which to compare it.

That is the way it is with the great and precious promises of God.

A minister visited a dear old lady one day and thumbed through her Bible. He noticed that she had written the letters "T.P." almost everywhere in the Bible and asked her what these letters meant. She said, "Tried and proven."

God's promises are great because they are precious, and precious because they are great. They are without flaw or imperfection.

When that mighty missionary David Livingstone went to Glasgow University to receive the honorary Doctor of Laws degree he said, "Would you like for me to tell you what supported me through all the years of exile among people whose language I could not understand, and whose attitude toward me was always uncertain and often hostile? It was this, 'Lo, I am with you alway, even unto the end of the world.' " On this promise Livingstone staked everything, and of it he said, "It is the word of a gentleman of the most strict and sacred honor, so there's an end of it."

When he was found in the jungles of Africa on his knees, face in hands, cold in death, his Bible was opened to that text upon which he had placed his finger a thousand times.

The Bible gives us thousands upon thousands of exceeding great and precious promises. They are all tried and proven. God's justice makes it impossible for him not to keep his word. His grace will not allow him to forget and his truth will not suffer him to change. His power enables him to keep his promises.

God has ten thousand blessings for those who love him. Do not miss them. Lay hold on them today. As a check is no good unless it is cashed, so it is with the promises of God. God wants you to appropriate them. There is nothing too good for his children.

43

Priceless Jewel of the Soul

On any Lord's Day multiplied millions of people say consciously and unconsciously, "I'm not going to church today."

Two fellows went fishing one Sunday. One's conscience began to hurt him, so he said to his companion, "We should have gone to church today." His friend replied, "I couldn't have gone anyway because my wife is sick."

A moment's thought convinces us that such excuses as this are unreasonable. Worship is the priceless jewel of the soul. Rufus M. Jones says that worship is "the central act without which any person's religion will always remain dwarfed and unfilled."

One day a pastor visited a parishioner who had been staying away from church. As they sat by the fireside the church member said, "I have decided that I can worship just as well here at home." Without a word the pastor took the tongs and lifted a blazing log from the fire and laid it apart from the others. In a little while it ceased to blaze and became a charred and black stick of wood. Pointing to it, the pastor said, "That is what happens when you stay away from the church. When you lose the kindling warmth of Christian fellowship, the fire goes down, the heart grows cold, and instead of spiritual warmth and cheer there remain the dull ashes of a dead spiritual hope."

William Lyons Phelps, who for many years taught at Yale University, once declared, "I would rather belong to the church than belong to any other organization or society or club. I would rather be a church member than receive any honor or decoration."

The best people in the world are church people. Most of the great and good people of the world were brought up in the church. Our Savior loved the church and gave himself for it. You and I should love him and want to be loyal and true to the agency of which he is the supreme head and against which hell has no power.

Why should we go on drinking at broken cisterns and empty wells when through worship God quenches the thirst and satisfies the hunger of our souls? Let us then exclaim with the psalmist, "I was glad when they said unto me, Let us go into the house of the Lord" (122:1).

44

Who Carries the Devil's Business On?

What is happening to our national morals?

This question is being asked by pulpit and press alike. On January 15, 1965, *The San Francisco Examiner* answered this question by saying:

An educator speaks out in favor of free love.

A man of God condones sexual excursions by unmarried adults.

Movies sell sex as a commercial commodity.

Book stores and cigar stands peddle pornography.

A high court labels yesterday's smut as today's literature.

Record shops feature albums featuring nudes and near nudes.

Night clubs stage shows that would have shocked a smoker audience a generation ago.

TV shows put out a flood of sick, sadistic and suggestive sex situations.

A campaign is launched to bring homosexuality to acceptability.

Radio broadcasts present discussions for and against promiscuity.

Magazines and newspapers publish pictures and articles that flagrantly violate the bonds of good taste.

Four letter words once heard in barroom brawls now appear in publications of general distribution.

Birth control counsel is urged for high school girls.

Something has gone wrong with the past principles of decency and good taste. Long long ago an ancient writer declared, "There is none that doeth good, no, not one. Their throat is an open sepulchre; with their tongues they have used deceit; the poison of asps is under their lips: whose mouth is full of cursing and bitterness: their feet are swift to shed blood: destruction and misery are in their ways: and the way of peace have they not known: there is no fear of God before their eyes" (Rom. 3:12–18).

There is no cruelty man will not inflict, no outrage he will not commit, no brutality he will not practice, and no depth of infamy to which he will not descend. All the butcheries and brutalities the world has ever known are being reenacted in our world today.

One of the great preachers of the past, Robert Hall, once imagined a celestial messenger coming to earth to study man in order to report back to heaven. "What will this celestial messenger say?" asked the man of God. "He will say this is not earth, this is hell! This is not man, but a demon tormenting demon."

No wonder Pascal once exclaimed, "What a chimera is man! What a subject of contradiction! What a confused chaos! A feeble worm of the earth! A mere huddle of uncertainty; the glory and the scandal of the universe."

One of the poets tells us:

> Some folks don't believe in a devil now,
> As our fathers use to do . . .
>
> But simple folks (like you and me) would like to know
> Who carries his business on?

"There is no fear of God before their eyes."

45

Don't Let God Be a Stranger in Your Life

If we are realistic when we lift the cover off the world about us, we readily admit that in many ways it is no better than it was a thousand or ten thousand years ago.

If someone who died ten thousand years ago were to come back to earth, and the people were removed so that as he went up and down the land he saw only the marvelous achievements of our age, he would say, "This is not the world that I once lived in." But if the people were called back and he saw how they lived, he would declare, "This is the same world in which I once lived, the same kind of people with the same old sins."

Man was born in sin; he is a sinner by nature and by practice. If this is not so, then half or more of what goes on in our world is without reason.

Jesus knew what was in man; he said, "Out of the heart proceed evil thoughts, murders, adulteries, fornications, thefts, false witness, blasphemies" (Matt. 15:19). Man's heart is a menagerie of evil beasts; a brood of demons lives there. The devil may be voted out by some people, but he lacks a lot being dead. He's the liveliest creature abroad in our world today.

We are witnessing today the steady erosion of moral principles which have been the foundation of civilization. As moral standards sink lower and lower, crime, juvenile delinquency, and social problems rise higher and higher. There is a higher percentage of young people in jail, on probation, or in trouble today than ever before. Statistics on illegitimate births, social diseases, broken marriages, sex deviation, alcoholism, dope addiction, and crimes of passion are appalling.

Where will all of this end? Is the human race hopelessly depraved? Is there no cure? If so, where? Can anything change man? What is the answer?

Is it education? Education may enlighten us, but it cannot save us. A set of idiots could not have done worse with some of the messes we have in our world. Some men reputed to be scholarly and cultured have been beastly. Education is not the answer.

Can science save us? Science may teach us many things about God, but it also increases our capacity for brutality and equips us for murder on a wholesale scale. Science cannot and does not save. In fact, Dr. Arthur Compton says, "Science has created a world in which Christianity is imperative."

Can the law save us? We have found that although men build peace palaces at the cost of millions and write pacts to guarantee the peace of the world, they are often no more than scraps of paper to be trampled under by godless nations.

Someone has given us this formula: "God added to this world makes peace; God added to human life makes happiness. God subtracted from this wicked world leaves war; God subtracted from human life leaves hell."

What we need is not so much reformation as it is regeneration. New birth can change our lives. "Verily, verily I say unto thee," said Jesus, "Except a man be born again he cannot see the kingdom of God" (John 3:3).

"As Moses lifted up the serpent in the wilderness, even so must the Son of man be lifted up: that whosoever believeth in him should not perish, but have eternal life" (John 3:14–15).

Don't let God be a stranger in your life.

46

Conquering Inner Space

We are living in the "space rage." The United States is enjoying tremendous success in conquering outer space. The control of space, according to scientists, means control of the world. Whoever gains that ultimate position, they tell us, gains total control over the earth for purposes of tyranny or for the service of freedom.

British astronomer Angus Armitage estimates that man has lived upon the earth for a quarter of a million years. He says there are five stages of human adventure: the Agricultural Man, the Mechanical Man, the Religious Man, the Political Man, and the Scientific Man.

To these five stages has been added a sixth, which may be called the Space Man.

Man has climbed a long way from nomadic savagery to an age when satellites encircle our globe at the fantastic speed of seventeen or eighteen thousand miles an hour, and man lands and walks on the moon.

This is not the end. Some of our brainiest men tell us that we will land a man on Mars by the 1980s. We wonder what the future holds. Space Man has created an atmosphere which, in the words of John Donne, is "pregnant with the old twins, Hope and Fear."

The story is told of an Arab who sent his sons out into the world to get what learning they could. After four years they came home, and he took them into the desert and showed them a strange sight. "What is that?" he asked his eldest son. "Why, the bones of a tiger," was the reply, "and his age when he died," explained the son as he examined the bones, "was seven years and three months, and his length from the tip of his tail to the tip of his nose was seven feet nine inches."

The father, greatly impressed that his son had learned so much, turned to his second son and asked, "What can you do?" The second son went to work and built up the skeleton of the tiger and set it on the desert sand.

Even more surprised the father asked the third son what he could do. The third son stuffed the tiger, covered it with skin, and put eyes in its head.

"There is nothing more to be done," said the father. He wondered how he could test the fourth son, but before he could speak, the fourth son said, "Wait a minute," and he stood in front of the tiger, uttered magic words, and sent a spark from the tip of his finger into the tip of the tiger's nose. The tiger rolled his eyes, life surged through his body, he opened his mouth, and making a mighty leap he ate them all up!

Will this nuclear space age end all human adventure? Who knows?

While Uncle Sam spends billions of dollars shooting for the moon, there are millions upon millions of people on earth who perish, not only with physical hunger, but also because they have little knowledge of God. As important as the control of outer space is, there is something of far greatest importance, and that is that we learn to control our wild and savage world. Our greatest need is a great spiritual thrust into inner space.

Only as men are brought into a knowledge of God through Christ will there be any tomorrow. Man's latent power must be turned into constructive good. The seventh stage of man's development must be the *Spiritual Man.*

47

The Touch of Your Hand

When a theological student in Boston, I was privileged to meet and hear the great poet Edwin Markham quote his "Man with a Hoe" and other poems. Markham had a deep sympathy and understanding of the suffering, the heartaches, the sorrows, the loneliness and burdens of the human race.

One of his poems which touches me the deepest is called "Bring Me Your Tears":

> I dare not ask your very all:
> I only ask a part.
> Bring me, when dancers leave the hall,
> Your aching heart.
> Give other friends your lighted face,
> The laughter of the years:
> I come to crave a greater grace:
> Bring me your tears!

Thomas Carlyle once said, "A great, deep, genuine sincerity is the first characteristic of any man who in any way can be called great." There can be no time for true greatness unless there is time for genuine sympathy.

The world hungers for love, sympathy, and understanding, and if there has ever been a time in history for these characteristics, it is now.

Some years ago I was in great sorrow. Many friends came and there were flowers, letters, and telegrams. One of the messages that comforted me the most and which I have remembered the longest came from a friend who had recently traveled this path. He said simply, "I understand." Isn't that what we all need—someone who understands?

One day a young minister got off a train in Cleveland and saw a blind, crippled soldier on crutches, carrying a heavy suitcase. He immediately offered to carry the suitcase, but the soldier wouldn't let him.

"Then may I guide you up the stairs to the station?" asked the minister.

"Yes, if you will," replied the soldier.

When they got to the top of the stairs the minister said, "Now, where do you want to go?"

"To the information desk, please," he replied.

The young preacher took a firm and rather possessive hold on the soldier's arm. Much to his surprise the blind, crippled war hero jerked his arm away and said abruptly: "Don't take possession of me, pal, and don't shove me. All I want is just the touch of your hand on my shoulder."

There are plenty of people in this troubled world who need help, but they don't want to be considered helpless. They don't want to be babied. All they want is just a touch of your hand on their shoulders and to know that you understand.

48

Maintaining the Spiritual Glow

Charles Lamb once said, "Our spirits grow gray before our hairs." One of the saddest things that can happen to us is to lose our zest for living. Nothing—not wealth, fame, honor, pleasure, or achievement—can take the place of the joy that comes from the romance of great living.

How quickly the freshness of life passes away for some people! One starts with the glow of life in his heart. He gazes down the coming years with the spirit of an adventurer, but ere he has traveled far life blows its winds upon him. The storms come and the rains descend and, disillusioned over his dreams, he plods wearily over a pathway from which glory has departed. Hopes and ambitions which once spurred him are now lifeless. Far horizons no longer beckon, joy flees, and life becomes hollow and miserable.

Why is it that some who have been beaten and battered by life are able to rise and conquer, while others merely fall by the wayside? What makes the difference? An old sign in a print shop reads: "Life is a grindstone and whether it grind a man down or polishes him up depends on the stuff he's made of." No man is defeated until he is defeated inside.

"The fault, dear Brutus, is not in the stars, but in ourselves," says Cassius. We blame everybody but ourselves.

A farmer was having a hard time with his wagon. It was tough going, so he called to a man by the roadside, "How much longer does this hill last?"

"Hill? This is no hill. Your hind wheels are off!"

There are some things that we can do to maintain our zest for living. We cannot control the length of our lives but we can control their width and depth. We cannot control the weather but we can control the moral atmosphere about us. "Our primary task," says a famous psychologist, "is not to fit a man to face his environment, but to fit him to face himself." And no person can ever manage himself until he comes to terms with himself and with God.

Life's greatest adventure is the adventure of living, and life's noblest achievement is the continual remaking of oneself so that one knows how to live.

> To every one there openeth
> A way and ways and a way,
> And every man decideth
> The way his soul shall go.

A young airman who was doing his solo flying for the first time got into serious trouble before making his landing. After the grave hour had passed, he filled out the log of his flight. In the space provided for listing his passengers he wrote, "God."

If we would maintain the spiritual glow and not lose the zest for great living, we must have God in Christ as a passenger on our ship.

49

Crippling the Church

One of the saddest scenes in the life of our Lord took place during the last Passover meal in the upper room. If the disciples should ever have been in harmony, it was then.

This was the hour of crisis. Jesus faced unimaginable suffering and certain death. But one of his disciples was a traitor. Judas had already bargained to sell him into the hands of enemies for thirty pieces of silver.

Most people think that Christ's worst enemies are outside the church. This is not true. History reveals that the enemies of Christianity cannot destroy it. Christianity thrives on persecution. The catacombs of Rome illustrate this. Christianity goes on! It cannot be stamped out.

The enemies that do the church the most damage are not those on the outside but some who are on the inside. Judas was on the inside. He was considered a friend of Jesus. Some of the most disastrous events in Christian history did not come from Christ's opponents but from worshipers who said, "Lord, Lord."

Some of us would never betray Christ as Judas did, but it might be well for us to think of some of the lesser ways in which we cripple the church. Some of these ways are unintentional, of course, but nonetheless they help to kill rather than to build the church. What are some of these ways?

1. By moving into another town or city and not transferring our church membership.

2. By putting everything else ahead of our church.

3. By staying home during church services.

4. By attending Sunday School and not staying for worship service.

5. By finding fault with everything the church does.

6. By leaving the impression with our children that the church is not important when, as a matter of fact, nothing else matters so much.

7. By never inviting anyone to attend the services of our church.

8. By never praying for the pastor and other members.

9. By never seeking to win a soul to Christ.

10. By thinking we are better than everybody else.

11. By never giving anything to the church.

12. By letting the other fellow do everything that needs to be done.

13. By living like saints on Sunday and devils during the week.

John Bunyan once said, "I have looked the whole thing in the face; and cost what it may, I mean to have Christlikeness and will." People who have Christlikeness are different. They outpray, outlove, outlive, and outwork the pagan world. They build and do not kill the influence of their churches by any sort of disloyalty. They who are most like Christ are faithful to the end.

Imagine Christ saying to us, "One of you shall betray me." Let us ask ourselves, "Lord, is it I?"

50

There's Power in Prayer!

Prayer is the mightiest force on earth. There just isn't anything comparable. It changes lives.

A few years ago I led a party into St. Giles' Cathedral in the beautiful city of Edinburgh. Instead of a spire this church, where the kings and queens of Scotland have worshiped, wears a crown. It is the church where the mighty John Knox preached, of whom it is said that the Queeen of Scotland feared his prayers more than she feared invading armies.

I said to our guide, "Can you tell me where John Knox knelt to pray?" I'm not sure that he knew what I was talking about but he pointed to a place near the high, exquisitely beautiful pulpit. Our entire party knelt and prayed where we thought Knox had prayed.

We can't always pray where Knox prayed, but each person may have his own place of prayer, and each of us, if we will, may pray without ceasing. Waiting hours thus spent are not wasted hours. Jesus said that "men ought always to pray, and not to faint" (Luke 18:1). Couldn't we use the time spent waiting for a red light to change or for an elevator in some hospital or skyscaper to talk to God and to let God talk to us? Martin Luther said that he was such a busy man that he had to spend four hours a day in prayer. Satan trembles when he sees even the weakest saint upon his knees!

The best advice I ever received was from my pastor as I was leaving home to go to college to study for the ministry. He said, "James, get you a little rug and place it by your bed and wear it out on your knees."

Believe it or not, I tried it. I prayed my way through college and the seminary and every step of the way. I humbly confess that I could not possibly carry the heavy burdens and responsibilities that each day brings in a great city pastorate were it not for the power of prayer.

I am just old-fashioned enough to believe that if Abraham's prayers saved Lot, if Moses' prayers brought manna from heaven and water out of a dry rock, if Jacob prayed and became a prince in Israel, if Joseph's prayers became altar stairs to a throne in Egypt, if Joshua prayed his way into the Promised Land, if Elisha prayed and God spared the widow's son, if Isaiah's prayers stayed Judah's downfall, if Daniel prayed and God closed the mouths of hungry lions, if the three Hebrew children prayed their way through a fiery furnace, if Jonah prayed and God spared Nineveh, if Hannah prayed Israel's greatest judge into existence, if Hezekiah prayed and God added fifteen years to his life, if Solomon prayed and became one of the wisest men who ever lived, if Peter prayed and became a rock, if John prayed and saw the window of heaven open, if a dying thief prayed his way into paradise, if Stephen prayed and saw the glory of God, if the disciples prayed and Pentecost came and three thousand souls were saved, if Paul and Silas prayed their way out of jail, and if my Lord and Savior, Jesus Christ, thought prayer to be so important that he often spent all night in prayer, then, I repeat, I am old-fashioned enough to believe with all my heart that there is *power in prayer.*

51

Can We Avoid Our Doom?

In the fall of 1946 the great Winston Churchill surveyed the scenes all about him in Europe. Cities were in ruin. Millions of homes had been destroyed. "Is brotherhood any nearer?" he asked. "Old hatreds burn with undying flame. . . . skeletons with gleaming eyes glare at each other across the ashes and rubble heap. . . . Is there never to be an end? Is there no salvation here below? Are we to sink through gradations of infinite suffering to primordial levels—

> A discord. Dragons of the prime,
> That tear each other in their slime,

or can we avoid our doom?"

This is the question of the ages. It has been asked century after century. Is there any way out of the muddle? Is there salvation anywhere? Can we avoid our doom?

There is, deep in the human heart, that which refuses to take no for an answer. There is something invincible and indestructible in man. Man hopes. Even when the night is the blackest his song of hope is the loudest. He somehow believes there is a way to avoid his doom.

Many people think that knowledge is the answer. It dispels ignorance, overcomes prejudice, raises the standard of living, broadens and elevates the minds of men, and refines and enriches character.

Others think that legislation, not knowledge, is the major cure for the ills of mankind. Legislation has a long and glorious list of achievements to its credit.

But the problem goes much deeper than either education or legislation. There is one thing fundamentally wrong with human nature: it is unregenerate and desperately needs to be regenerated. Herbert Spencer once said, "There is no political alchemy by which you get golden conduct out of leaden instincts." But there *is* the alchemy of the cross, which accomplishes just that.

This is the message of Christianity, the very heart of the gospel. It says that human nature can be changed—genuinely, radically, and permanently. The drunkard can become sober, the impure pure, the grouch genial, the miser generous, the crook upstanding. Christianity stands or falls by its claims to transform human nature. Someone has said, "If Jesus cannot make character, he can make nothing else."

This is why Hugh Redwood of the *London News* staff once said: "If you should ask me by what authority I talk about the power of Christ to change human nature, I should reply to you simply (and God knows without one thought of boasting), because he has changed my nature. I know that I am really and literally a new creature in Christ Jesus since the day he came into my life."

52

The Peril of Privilege

Set habitually among diamonds, a man may think of himself as a diamond when he may be only an imitation.

Jesus found that one of the most difficult problems ethically for man was privilege. It was the crux of his conflict with the Pharisees. They were a highly privileged people whose pride caused them to build a great, high wall around themselves, shutting them off from sympathy with common people. This Jesus detested.

The same Sunday that Chief Justice Charles Hughes of the United States Supreme Court moved his church membership to Washington, a Chinese laundryman also offered himself for membership. The pastor exclaimed, "The ground is wondrously level at the foot of the cross!"

But the ground is not so level for a lot of highly privileged people. There is no wall as high, wide, or long as privileged position to shut out the pitiful cries of the poor, starving, suffering, sick, wounded humanity.

Privilege blinds people to the great wrongs that mar our world. Take this matter of poverty, for instance. Is it, as Mrs. Orville Schaefer, former head of Georgia's State Welfare Department, says, merely a "faceless, ill-defined condition that most of us simply shudder over, and think of something else—something more pleasant"?

Poverty has a face and a personality. It is so easy to see this problem in terms of statistics only; but if we are to be a part of its solution, we must see more than figures. We must see faces.

Mrs. Schaefer well reminds us that one of the first things we must do is to break down the barriers between those who enjoy the fruits of progress and prosperity and those who make up the impoverished one fifth of our population. "We cannot," she says, "wall ourselves off from these people who exist in poverty and need."

"For unto whomsoever much is given, of him shall be much required," Jesus said (Luke 12:48).

Privilege unselfishly possessed, humbly dedicated, and sacrificially renounced is one of the noblest and most beautiful things in all the world. This is the ethical core of Christianity.

"He that is greatest among you shall be your servant. And whosoever shall exalt himself shall be abased; and he that shall humble himself shall be exalted" (Matt. 23:12).

53

Does Everything Always Happen for the Best?

His wife had just died and he was left with three little children to care for. He was not bitter, but sad and lonely. Some of his friends tried to comfort him by saying, "You will find that it was all for the best."

No matter how hard he tried, he just couldn't see it that way. He felt deeply that she meant far more to the welfare of the family than he, even though he was their breadwinner. He could not and would not say that it was for the best, and he wondered how anyone else could.

Does everything always happen for the best? Many believe so. But there are those who ask, "How can you say that everything—things like crime, like millions being killed or wounded at war, poverty, blindness, sickness, suffering, and old age—always turn out for the best?"

Does the Bible teach this? The answer is no.

The Bible does teach something similar to this in one of its most beautiful verses, Romans 8:28, where it says, "We know that all things work together for good to them that love God, to them who are the called according to his purpose." It tells us that all things work together for *good,* not for the best. There is a distinction. The blessed assurance is not necessarily an assurance of the absolute best, but of some positive good.

The good that comes is based upon two conditions: it comes "to them that love God," and "to them who are the called according to his purpose." All things are not inherently good, neither do all things of themselves produce good. Nor do all things work together to produce good to all people. But all things work together for good to those who respond to God's call, who love and put their trust in him.

As an architect may for many reasons have to alter his original plan, so the Supreme Architect of the universe may for various reasons have to revise his plan for our little lives; but for those who meet the conditions good will always come.

I shall never forget the day our good doctor told us that my mother had only a little while to live. When I retired that night I slept an hour or two and then suddenly and startlingly awakened to enter Gethsemane. I thought my heart would burst. I slipped quietly into my study, fell on my knees, and cried like a baby.

Unable to sleep, I decided to clear off my desk. In a moment or two I found a birthday card from my mother with Romans 8:28 printed on it. It comforted my aching heart. I said, "This is my mother's faith. She believes it." Then I kept on at my desk and soon came across another card from my mother. It had the same text on it. Once again I fell to my knees and said, "Thank you, God. I do not know the meaning of it all, but I do know I love you and am called according to your purpose, and if this text is good enough for my mother it is good enough for me. I'll trust everything to you."

What has life done to you? Has something happened in your life that you do not understand? Have you known some great disappointment? Whatever it is, keep on loving and trusting and doing your best for God and God will see that good comes out of it.

54

What to Do When You Fumble the Ball

Who among us has never fumbled the ball? Only a fool says, "I have never made a mistake." To err is human. No man compliments himself when he declares he has never blundered. The person who has never made a mistake has probably never made anything. It is vastly better for us to make some mistakes in life and do something than to make no mistakes and do nothing. The person who has never fumbled the ball has never won any victories.

In fact, the greatest people the world has ever known made grave mistakes. There is not an outstanding merchant, lawyer, doctor, professor, banker, farmer, judge, politician, military leader, or preacher who has never made an error. Some of our mistakes are known only to ourselves. We hang our heads in shame over them. If we could retrace the way we have come, we could change many things.

Since we cannot go back, what then shall we do? Shall we grieve unduly? It does us good to fail sometimes. To feel that we have not done so well may cause us to fight the game harder. "Low aim, not failure, is crime." Our mistakes can be stepping stones to higher plateaus.

Cicero once said, "Any man may commit a mistake, but none but a fool will continue in it." The same thought is expressed in an old Spanish proverb that says, "He is a fool who stumbles over the same stone." And in the words of a recent president of Atlanta's Bar Association, "There is no education in the second kick of a mule."

If we have been kicked once, let's not be kicked again. If we have stumbled over a stone, let's not stumble over the same stone twice. Let's forget the mistakes of the past and, as Paul did, "press toward the mark for the prize of the high calling of God in Christ Jesus."

In James Morgan's biography of Abraham Lincoln we find the story of a soldier who was condemned to die in a camp near Washington because he had fallen asleep while on guard duty. The offense was particularly serious because the safety of the Capitol depended on the watchfulness of the sentries. The officials were determined to make an example out of this green lad from Vermont. Every effort to save him failed until the captain and other members of his company, all neighbors of the doomed officer, went to the White House and pled with President Lincoln on his behalf.

Lincoln, in great magnanimity of heart, visited the boy and inquired about his parents. The boy told the story of his simple home among the hills and showed Mr. Lincoln a picture of his parents. President Lincoln himself had been brought up on a farm and knew how hard it was for a country boy to keep awake at night, especially when new to army habits and duties. Thinking the lad too good a boy to be shot for merely falling asleep once, he promised to free him, but at a heavy cost. His parents must mortgage their farm for him, and the boy alone would pay the bill by proving himself as brave and faithful as any soldier in the Union. The boy's face brightened. The President's hand rested on his shoulder, and the boy pledged that he would not disappoint him.

The bill was presented in the Peninsular Campaign. It was the boy's first and last battle. He was the first to face the blazing rifles of the Confederates, plunging into the water again and again under shot of the foe, rescuing his wounded comrades until he had brought back the last of them, but with a bullet in his own heart.

117

He paid his bill in full and died blessing the mercy of Abraham Lincoln for trusting him and letting him serve with honor.

However we fumble the ball in life, if we are truly penitent, the Lord of all would tell us as Lincoln did this soldier, "Wake up, get back to your posts of duty, and fight."

55

The Love of a Friend

In the will of an associate justice of the United States Supreme Court who died some years ago were these words: "Friendships are the most cherished and prized possession of our life and too often among the rarest; they are greater than gold or gear. They figure most prominently in last wills and testaments and they often take longer to create than large estates. A fortune may be gotten in a day, on the turn of a card, as it were—but not a friendship. That takes time."

How true this is!

Elizabeth Browning once asked the sainted Charles Kingsley, "What is the secret of your life? Tell me that I may make mine beautiful, too." Kingsley replied, "I had a friend."

If, like Mrs. Browning, we want our lives to be beautiful, we must make them friendly. The only way to have a friend is to be a friend. The people who have the most friends are those who lose themselves in unselfish service to others. Such lives add much to the world's wealth. No amount of money can ever buy or recompense them. They are worth far more than silver or gold.

If our lives are to be really radiant and useful, we too must have a friend—the Friend of all friends, Jesus Christ. His is the highest, holiest, and grandest friendship of all. He wants to be our friend. He says, "Greater love hath no man than this, that a man lay down his life for his friends. Ye are my friends, if ye do whatsoever I command you. Henceforth I call you not servants; . . . but I have called you friends" (John 15:13–15).

Many years ago I spent some time in the library of Furman University and came to know Dr. O. O. Fletcher, author of one of the first introductions to philosophy to be taught in the South.

When about to depart, I went by to tell this great man good-bye and to thank him for his kindness to me. It was the last time I ever say him, and he gave me an everlasting blessing. With tears in his eyes, he quoted one of his favorite poems, called "The Love of a Friend." This I pass on to you with the prayer that it may bless you as it has blessed me:

> Like music on still waters,
>> Like pines when the wind passeth by,
> Like pearls in the deep of the ocean,
>> Like stars which enamel the sky,
> Like June and the odor of roses,
>> Like dew and the freshness of morn,
> Like sunshine which kisses the clover,
>> Like tassels of silk on the corn,
> Like notes of thrush in the woodland,
>> Like brooks where violets grow,
> Like rainbows that arch the blue heaven,
>> Like clouds when the sun dippeth low,
> Like dreams of Arcadian pleasure,
>> Like colors which gracefully blend,
> Like everything breathing of pureness,
>> Like these is the love of a friend.

56

Music Out of Life's Remainders

If we could draw back the curtains and look into heaven, we could see a great multitude around the white throne of God—a multitude of all nations, kindreds, peoples, and tongues, clothed in white robes, palms in their hands, and singing at the tops of their voices.

We are told that "these are they which came out of great tribulation, and have washed their robes, and made them white in the blood of the Lamb" (Rev. 7:14).

The word tribulation literally means "pressure." These people in heaven had lived their lives under severe pressure, opposition, difficulty, disadvantage, and encumbrances. To endure such pressure is the only way into the kingdom of God.

Perhaps you never thought of it, but biography proves that all people are handicapped in some way or another. The secret quality of one's spiritual life depends on the way he handles his handicap.

Did you know that William the Conqueror, Alexander the Great, Alexander Hamilton, Leonardo da Vinci, Borodin, James Smithson, and Booker T. Washington were, according to Frederick J. Haskins, all of illegitimate birth?

Perhaps you didn't know that Louis Pasteur, France's great scientist who laid the foundations for modern medicine, had a paralytic stroke at the age of forty-six and was handicapped the rest of his life.

You may not have remembered that Beethoven was deaf and John Milton, blind; that Gamaliel Bradford was limited to 120 minutes of work a day as an invalid, or that Charles Lamb gave up the thought of marriage to care for a sister who in a fit of insanity murdered their mother.

Many years ago that eminent Philadelphia preacher, Russell H. Conwell, analyzed the lives of 4,043 American millionaires and found that all but twenty of them started out as poor boys.

B. C. Forbes tells us that out of fifty of America's biggest businessmen, twenty-four were born poor, seventeen in moderate circumstances, and only nine were born rich.

So, we may safely repeat that everybody has some kind of handicap.

The question that concerns us is, what are we going to do with them? The wise person accepts and uses them as challenging opportunities.

When Paganini made his first appearance before the aristocracy of Paris, a strange thing happened. As he began to tune his violin, one string snapped and the audience tittered. He tried again and another string broke. A moment later a third one gave way. By now the audience was laughing aloud, but Paganini did not lose his poise. With a pleasant smile he put his violin to his chin and brought forth music from that one remaining string that thrilled the waiting throng.

How wonderful it is when one brings music out of life's remainders!

57

The World in Crisis

The world is in crisis today.

On every hand our world is being challenged by international Communism, the population explosion, civil strife, and technological revolution.

The crisis is an economic one; whoever controls the world's economy may control the world.

The crisis is also military, for upon which side has the greatest militar might, the safety of the rest of the world depends.

Likewise, the crisis is political, for the battle between the totalitarian and the free systems is fierce.

Finally, our world crisis is scientific, for what can be more significant for the future than the harnessing of nature's forces or the conquest of space. In this day when astronauts and cosmonauts attempt to reach the moon, many questions are being asked, some even daring to ask, "Will we lose God in outer space?"

The present crisis has many facets, but in its deepest dimension it is more than an economic, military, political, or scientific dilemma—it is spiritual. It has to do with the age-old problem of sin. It has to do with God and how well people know, love, honor, and serve him. When men come to love God with all of their hearts, souls, and minds, all of these other matters will take care of themselves. Upon the crisis of God every other crisis depends.

It is tragic indeed to be flippant, superficial, or indifferent about it.

It is folly to think that half-hearted measures will avail.

It is unpardonable to do nothing. The way for evil to triumph is for good men to remain silent.

On a recent trip abroad I visited thirty-one of our foreign missionaries in their homes and on their fields of work in many lands. I asked one of them in a Moslem country, "What is the answer to all of these revolutions you have here? What is the answer to downtrodden womanhood and childhood, lack of sanitation, ignorance, and superstition? Why are people satisfied to live in mud huts? Tell me," I insisted, "what is the answer to all this?"

Without a moment's hesitation and with the radiance of heaven upon his face, this man exclaimed, "Christ! Christ is the only answer! Only as people come to know Christ will there be a change in our world."

If we settle the spiritual crisis of our world, the rest will take care of itself.

58

Why I Have Not Quit the Ministry

On November 17, 1962, there appeared in *The Saturday Evening Post* under the cloak of anonymity an article entitled "Why I Quit the Ministry," in which a minister tells quite frankly the painful story of why he quit. Since this article appeared, many ministers throughout the world, including myself, have doubtless given thought to the reasons why they have not quit.

First, let's take a look at some of the reasons the Reverend Mr. Anonymous gives. He complained that people didn't want to hear Christ's idea of Christianity. Four fifths of his church members gave almost nothing. Some who lived in very expensive homes gave only a "tip." A clique ruled the church. Some members walked out when two well-dressed Negroes attended. The church members were more interested in their social schedule than in Christian service. One couple got a divorce and a brilliant young engineer became an alcoholic. A dozen teen-agers were sexually promiscuous. The Sunday School teachers didn't want to improve themselves or the educational program. The church was not interested in developing spiritually. Out of eight hundred members only half of them ever attended, even periodically. The majority of the church members refused to care.

"This," he stated, "was not the ministry to which I had felt a call. How then," he continued, "can a minister rationalize devoting his life to the organization which results, a superficial extension of society? How can he live with himself if he does?" Thus he gave up the ministry.

My ministry has been a very happy one. It is a big job and, without God's help, I would not be equal to it, but oh! how I love it! It is my very life. To take me out of it would be like taking a fish out of water.

While I have failed many times as a preacher and pastor, I have always been conscious of having a loyal congregation behind me to love and pray for me. I have found most people to be kind, generous, gracious, and sympathetic. Most of my members have been my intimate friends, even like members of my own family.

Like the apostle Paul I can say that I was "made a minister," that I received my ministry from the Lord Jesus. Through all these years in the pastorate I have been deeply conscious of my divine commission. There isn't anything in the world that gives a minister more courage, power, confidence, and poise than the overwhelming conviction that he has received a supernatural, miraculous call. This is what gave Paul and the apostles and prophets such great power.

I don't think any man who is really called of God to preach can quit. If he does, he will be the most miserable man on earth.

This world that we're a-livin in
    Is mighty hard to beat;
You git a thorn with every rose,
    But ain't the roses sweet!